Compliments of

Boylan Code
Attorneys at Law

ROCHESTER

High Performance for 175 years

This page: Rochester skyline seen from the Genesee River with the Frederick Douglass–Susan B. Anthony Memorial Bridge and, from left to right, Chase Tower, Bausch & Lomb headquarters, and the Xerox Tower.

ROCHESTER

High Performance for 175 years

Robin L. Flanigan

This book was produced in cooperation with the City of Rochester, New York, and is the official commemorative publication celebrating Rochester's 175th anniversary. Cherbo Publishing Group gratefully acknowledges the city's important contribution to *Rochester: High Performance for 175 Years*.

cherbo publishing group, inc.

president	JACK C. CHERBO
chief operating officer	ELAINE HOFFMAN
editorial director	CHRISTINA M. BEAUSANG
managing feature editor	MARGARET L. MARTIN
feature editor	JO ELLEN KRUMM
senior profiles editor	J. KELLEY YOUNGER
profiles editors	NEVAIR KABAKIAN
	LIZA YETENEKIAN SMITH
associate editors	SYLVIA EMRICH-TOMA
	JENNY KORNFELD
editorial assistant/proofreader	MARK K. NISHIMURA
profiles writers	B. D. CAMPBELL
	SYLVIA EMRICH-TOMA
	NEVAIR KABAKIAN
	JENNY KORNFELD
	JO ELLEN KRUMM
creative director	PERI A. HOLGUIN
senior designer	THEODORE E. YEAGER
designer	NELSON CAMPOS
senior photo editor	WALTER MLADINA
photo editor	KAREN MAZE
digital color specialist	ART VASQUEZ
sales administrator	JOAN K. BAKER
client services supervisor	PATRICIA DE LEONARD
senior client services coordinator	LESLIE E. SHAW
client services coordinator	KENYA HICKS
executive assistant	JUDY ROBITSCHEK
administrative assistant	BILL WAY
regional development manager	GLEN EDWARDS
eastern regional manager	MARCIA WEISS
publisher's representative	LINDA SPROEHNLE

Cherbo Publishing Group, Inc.
Encino, California 91316

Printed in Canada
By Friesens

Subsidiary Production Office
Santa Rosa, CA, USA
888.340.6049

Library of Congress Cataloging-in-Publication data
Flanigan, Robin L.
A pictorial guide highlighting Rochester's economic and social advantages.

Library of Congress Control Number 2008941944
ISBN 978-1-882933-11-2
Visit the CPG Web site at www.cherbopub.com.

To purchase additional copies of this book, contact Joan Baker at Cherbo Publishing Group: jbaker@cherbopub.com or phone 818.783.0040 ext. 27.

Opposite page: Charlotte-Genesee Lighthouse.

Dedication

To Patrick, for bringing me to your hometown.

Acknowledgments

I gratefully acknowledge contributions by Ellen Rosen at Rochester Business Alliance and Staci Henning at Greater Rochester Enterprise for their contributions to *Rochester: High Performance for 175 Years.*

—Robin L. Flanigan

This page: Mount Hope Cemetery.

TABLE OF CONTENTS

L'ARTIGIANA

Left to right: Rochester International Jazz Festival; Lilac Festival; M&T Bank Clothesline Festival.

Rochester Museum & Science Center

Left to right: Rochester Contemporary Art Center; Memorial Art Gallery of the University of Rochester.

CORPORATIONS & ORGANIZATIONS PROFILED

The following organizations have made a valuable commitment to the quality of this publication.

BUSINESS VISIONARIES

The following companies and organizations are recognized as innovators in their fields and have played a prominent role in this publication, as they have in the region.

Boylan Brown
Growth.Protection.Succession.
BUSINESS AND CORPORATE LAW

Boylan, Brown, Code, Vigdor & Wilson, LLP
2400 Chase Square, Rochester, NY 14604
Contact: Robert E. Brown, Partner and CEO
Phone: 585-232-5300 / Fax: 585-232-3528
E-mail: rbrown@boylanbrown.com
Web site: www.boylanbrown.com

Clark Patterson Lee
DESIGN PROFESSIONALS

Clark Patterson Lee
205 St. Paul Street, Rochester, NY 14604
Todd M. Liebert, AIA, NCARB; President
Phone: 800-274-9000 / Fax: 585-454-7618
E-mail: tliebert@clarkpatterson.com
Web site: www.clarkpatterson.com
"Designing Around You"

The College at BROCKPORT
STATE UNIVERSITY OF NEW YORK

The College at Brockport, State University of New York
350 New Campus Drive, Brockport, NY 14420-2914
Contact: David Mihalyov, Executive Director of Public Relations
Phone: 585-395-2754
E-mail: dmihalyo@brockport.edu
Web site: www.brockport.edu

Constellation

Constellation Brands, Inc.
370 Woodcliff Drive, Suite 300, Fairport, NY 14450
Rob Sands, President and CEO
Phone: 585-218-3600 / Fax: 585-218-3800
Web site: www.cbrands.com

HARRIS
assuredcommunications®

Harris Corporation
RF Communications Division
1680 University Avenue, Rochester, NY 14610
Phone: 585-244-5830 / Fax: 585-242-4755
E-mail: RFComm@harris.com
Web site: www.rfcomm.harris.com

Preferred care
An MVP Health Care Company

Preferred Care
220 Alexander Street, Rochester, NY 14607
Contact: Lisa Brubaker, Executive Vice President
Phone: 585-258-8674
E-mail: lbrubaker@preferredcare.org
Web site: www.preferredcare.org

RG&E
Always at Your Service

Rochester Gas and Electric Corporation
89 East Avenue, Rochester, NY 14649
Contact: Clyde A. Forbes, Manager, NYS Economic Development & Regional Communications
Phone: 585-771-6040 / Fax: 585-724-8691
E-mail: clyde_forbes@rge.com
Web site: www.rge.com

ROCHESTER GENERAL HOSPITAL

Rochester General Hospital
1425 Portland Avenue, Rochester, NY 14621
Phone: 585-922-4000
Web site: www.rochestergeneral.org

ROCHESTER RIVERSIDE CONVENTION CENTER

Rochester Riverside Convention Center
123 East Main Street, Rochester, NY 14604-1619
Joseph A. Floreano, CFE, Executive Director
Phone: 585-232-7200 or 800-856-1678 / Fax: 585-232-1510
E-mail: Jfloreano@rrcc.com
Web site: www.rrcc.com
"We take care of all the details, so you can relax and enjoy your event."

Left to right: Java Wally's Café at the Rochester Institute of Technology Libraries; study time at The College at Brockport, State University of New York, with *Happiness for All the Children of the World* sculpture and fountain honoring the Special Olympics in the background.

Left to right: Dan Collins of the Rochester Americans hockey team greeting young fans; kayaking on the Genesee River in Lower Falls Park; Lorena Ochoa of Mexico competing in the 2008 Wegmans Rochester LPGA tournament, held at the Locust Hill Country Club.

FOREWORD

The inscription on Colonel Nathaniel Rochester's headstone in Mount Hope Cemetery, translated from the Latin, tells visitors, "If you seek his monument, look about you." The message is profound in its simplicity: The city itself is the most enduring legacy of our founder's bold enterprise.

The village Colonel Rochester settled in the years immediately after the Revolutionary War went on to become America's first boomtown as the Erie Canal opened the country's heartland to the commerce of the East Coast and Europe. Then, as now, it was infrastructure that drove Rochester's growth. But the challenges Rochester faced at the turn of the 19th century differ from those of the early 21st century. Today, the notion of infrastructure applies to much more than physical structures like roads, bridges, and schools. While we do have plenty of those things in Rochester, our community also boasts a vast array of modern facilities, including university and corporate research centers that propel innovation and invention; a wide network of cultural institutions that sharpen the minds of our residents; and an abundance of natural and man-made attractions that enrich the quality of our lives each day.

We have all that and more in this beautiful city on the banks of the Genesee River and Lake Ontario. But it is our people who have created the most important component of our success. In Rochester you will find the most industrious and diligent workers in the world, a population of thinkers and doers eager to embrace challenge and seize opportunity.

It is in this context that I am so very pleased and proud to invite you to read this fine book, *Rochester: High Performance for 175 Years*. From these pages you will learn why so many people love this city, whether they were born here or moved here as adults; and how a confluence of pioneers, events, and geography shaped a community that is now uniquely situated to prosper in a world increasingly defined by change.

I am certain Colonel Rochester would be pleased.

Robert J. Duffy

Mayor Robert J. Duffy

Opposite page: Bausch & Lomb Place with, from left to right, Bausch & Lomb headquarters, Xerox Tower, and *Genesee Passage*, a steel sculpture by Albert Paley.

ROCHESTER TIMELINE

1788 | 1823 | 1829 | 1837

Nathaniel Rochester

1788 Oliver Phelps and Nathaniel Gorham sign a treaty with the Seneca Indians to purchase 2.6 million acres of land east of the Genesee River.

1803 Colonel Nathaniel Rochester, Major Charles Carroll, and Colonel William Fitzhugh purchase a 100-acre tract of land in Western New York along the Genesee River. It will take them four years to pay $1,750 for the land.

1811 The settlement is platted and the first lots sold. The town will soon be called Rochesterville, which will later be shortened to Rochester.

1817 A volunteer fire company is organized.

View of Erie Canal by John William Hill, 1829

1823 The section of the Erie Canal connecting Rochester to the Hudson River is completed. It will carry high volumes of goods eastward, making Rochester the nation's first boom-town. Mills powered by the Genesee River will produce enough flour that Rochester will earn the title "Flour City" as the largest flour-producing city in the world.

1827 The village's first public market, featuring livestock, produce, crafts, and dry goods, opens on the north side of the Main Street Bridge.

1829 The Rochester Athenaeum, a cultural center for Rochesterians, is founded. The center offers public lectures and debates and houses a library.

1834 Rochester is incorporated as a city.

1835 Brockport Collegiate Institute, which will eventually become The College at Brockport, State University of New York, is founded.

1837 The public market moves to Front Street.

1838 Mount Hope Cemetery is founded.

1843 Rochester dentist Dr. J. B. Beers develops the nation's first gold tooth.

1847 Frederick Douglass, a former slave, moves to Rochester and begins publishing the abolitionist newspaper *The North Star*.

1848 The Rochester Gas Light Company is founded; it has 80 customers.

1849 Absalom Bishop and Thayer Codding invent the fountain pen.

1849 The Underground Railroad, a vast network of people, both whites and African Americans, who help fugitive slaves escape to the North, spreads to what is now Mendon Ponds Park and other area locations.

1850

1850 The University of Rochester is founded as a Baptist-sponsored, all-male institution.

1853 John Jacob Bausch opens a small optical shop at Reynolds Arcade. Henry C. Lomb soon joins as a partner. Bausch & Lomb will become the world leader in eye care.

1853 Addy Van Slyck is hired as the city's first police chief at a salary of $900 per year.

1856 Hiram Sibley's telegraph company merges with other telegraph companies to become Western Union Telegraph Company.

1862 The city's first paid fire department is established.

1863 Colonel Patrick Henry O'Rorke of Rochester dies leading forces in the Battle of Gettysburg. The efforts of his brigade, which includes the 140th New York Infantry Regiment, are crucial to the Union victory in this critical battle of the Civil War.

1864

1864 Rochester City Hospital, now Rochester General Hospital, opens.

1866 Chili Seminary, now Roberts Wesleyan College, is founded.

1871 Geneseo Normal School holds its first classes. It will become the State University of New York (SUNY) Geneseo.

1872 Susan B. Anthony votes in a national election, claiming that the 14th Amendment gives her that right. She is arrested several days later and charged with casting an illegal vote.

Western Union employees, 1938

1880

1880 George Eastman begins manufacturing the first photographic dry plates in the United States. His inventions will revolutionize photography.

1880 Rochester City Hospital starts a nursing school, the third in the state and the 12th in the country.

1883 James Cutler patents the mail chute for dropping mail from the upper stories of buildings. The first chute is installed in the Elwood Building in Rochester.

1885 Henry Lomb, Max Lowenthal, and other Rochester businessmen establish the Mechanics Institute to provide needed technical training for skilled industrial workers.

1888 George Eastman launches his "Kodak Number One Box Camera" with the slogan, "You press the button, we do the rest."

1891 The Rochester Athenaeum merges with the Mechanics Institute.

1892

1892 Horticulturist John Dunbar starts Highland Park's lilac collection with 20 varieties.

1893 Seneca Park, designed by landscape architect Frederick Law Olmsted, opens. A year later Seneca Park Zoo opens.

Advertisement for Kodak Box Camera, 1889

1893 St. Bernard's School of Theology and Ministry is founded.

1896 Voting machines, which were first officially used in Lockport, New York, four years earlier, are used on a larger scale in Rochester.

ROCHESTER TIMELINE

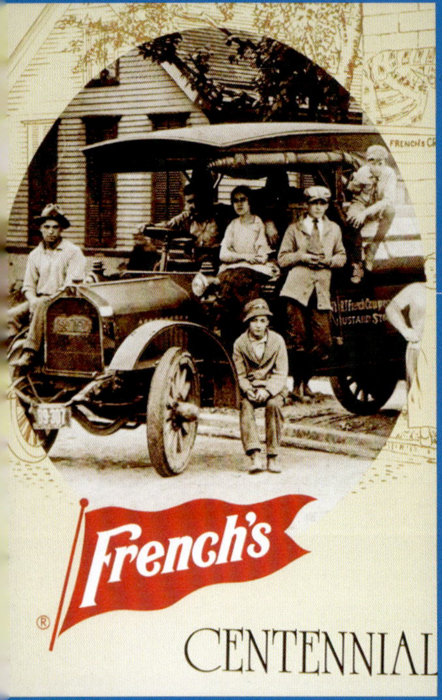

R. T. French advertisement from 2004 featuring Alphonse Street residents circa 1917

1898

1898 The Lilac Festival begins when 3,000 people gather informally one Sunday in May to see the lilacs in Highland Park.

1899 Hickey Freeman, a manufacturer of tailored men's clothing, is founded.

1900 Susan B. Anthony and Helen Barrett Montgomery persuade the University of Rochester to admit women.

1904 R. T. French Company in Rochester produces the first prepared mustard, which it introduces to the public at the St. Louis World's Fair.

1905 The public market moves once again, to its current site on North Union Street.

1906 The Haloid Company, which manufactures photographic paper and equipment, is founded. It will eventually become Xerox Corporation.

1907

1907 Cab Calloway, famed jazz singer and bandleader who is best known for the song "Minnie the Moocher," is born in Rochester.

1914 The 16-story Kodak Tower, Kodak's world headquarters, is built on the site of the old factory on State Street.

1916 John Wegman opens the Rochester Fruit & Vegetable Company. The company is later renamed Wegmans Food Markets.

1918 Frank Gannett and associates merge two newspapers into the *Rochester Times Union*. Five years later, Gannett buys out his associates and founds Gannett Co., which will eventually grow into an international communications giant and will become the nation's largest newspaper publisher.

1921 George Eastman establishes the Eastman School of Music, the first professional school of the University of Rochester.

1924

1924 Nazareth College is founded.

1926 Strong Memorial Hospital opens with one full-time faculty member and three pediatric house officers.

1928 Colgate and Rochester seminaries merge to create Colgate Rochester Divinity School.

1931 Fourteen area employers provide unemployment insurance for their employees, creating the first organized unemployment insurance plan in the nation.

1934 Arthur Wolfram Fuchs of the Eastman Kodak Company takes the first X-ray photograph of a living person's entire body in a one-second exposure.

1944 The Mechanics Institute becomes the Rochester Institute of Technology.

1945 Canandaigua Industries Company begins as a seller of bulk wine. It will become Constellation Brands, the largest wine producer in the world.

1945

John Lithgow

1945 Actor John Lithgow is born in Rochester. He will appear in films (*Terms of Endearment*), television shows (*3rd Rock from the Sun*), and Broadway shows (*M. Butterfly*).

1948 The city's first dial telephones are used by downtown Baker and Hamilton exchanges.

1948 St. John Fisher College is founded in Pittsford.

1948 1953 1971 1996

1948 The County of Monroe takes over Rochester Municipal Airport, renaming it Greater Rochester International Airport.

1949 The Haloid Company introduces the first xerographic (dry process) copy machine.

1952 Mount Morris Dam is built in Letchworth State Park to control flooding by the Genesee River.

Xerox Tower, 1980

1953 James A. Hard, the last surviving combat veteran of the Civil War, dies at the age of 111. He is the oldest male buried in Mount Hope Cemetery.

1961 The Haloid Company becomes Xerox Corporation.

1962 Midtown Plaza, the first downtown indoor shopping mall in the United States, opens.

1965 The New Liberty Pole, a 190-foot-high stainless-steel tower designed by Rochester architect James H. Johnson, is built downtown.

1968 The Xerox Tower, headquarters of Xerox Corporation, is completed. The 30-story, 443-foot building, is the tallest building in Rochester.

1971 Bausch & Lomb introduces the first soft contact lens.

1971 B. Thomas Golisano starts Paymaster, later renamed Paychex, to provide payroll to small businesses.

1974 The Statue of Mercury returns to the Rochester skyline as it is placed atop the Aqueduct Building. It originally graced a chimney at the Kimball Tobacco Factory from 1881 to 1951.

1978 Tim Redding, starting pitcher for Major League Baseball's Washington Nationals, is born in Rochester.

1982 Kodak introduces a line of cameras with disc film.

1983 Paychex becomes a publicly held company and constructs a new corporate headquarters on Panorama Trail South in Rochester.

1984 The old Charlotte-Genesee Lighthouse, constructed in 1822, opens as a museum.

1993 William A. Johnson Jr. is the first African American to be elected mayor of Rochester.

1996 Frontier Field, home to the Rochester Rhinos soccer team, opens.

2007 The Frederick Douglass–Susan B. Anthony Memorial Bridge, which carries Interstate 490 over the Genesee River and State Route 382, is dedicated. The award-winning design features a three-member steel arch structure that is the first of its kind in the United States.

2007 The 25th edition of the *Places Rated Almanac* lists Rochester number six of the Best Places to Live in America.

2008 After 46 years, most of Midtown Plaza closes. The center is slated for demolition in 2009, with a high-rise world headquarters for the communications company PAETEC Holding planned for the site.

Charlotte-Genesee Lighthouse

This page: The Rochester skyline, including the Frederick Douglass–Susan B. Anthony Memorial Bridge, from the Genesee River.

INVESTING IN THE FUTURE:
LIVING AND WORKING IN ROCHESTER

This page: The Frederick Douglass–Susan B. Anthony Memorial Bridge. Opposite page: Dancing Wings Butterfly Garden at the Strong National Museum of Play.

Quality of Life

THE IMAGE OF INNOVATION

Rochester, named for its cofounder, Colonel Nathaniel Rochester, an American Revolutionary War soldier and land speculator, was founded on an entrepreneurial spirit still prevalent today. New York's third-largest city—considered the nation's first boomtown—is situated on the Genesee River just south of Lake Ontario and is a community focused on investing in its future.

The region has a reputation for being family friendly and a good place to do business, earning top rankings in both mainstream and trade publications. The business journal *Expansion Management* named Rochester one of the "50 Hottest Cities for Business Expansion/Relocation" in 2006. *Places Rated Almanac* listed the metropolitan area sixth nationwide for best quality of life, taking into account such things as ambience, housing, and transportation. According to *Child* magazine, Rochester is one of the top 10 U.S. cities in which to raise a family. Public safety is a priority, and the city has a respected police department of more than 900 employees and a highly rated fire department of more than 500 employees. The area's Rochester–Monroe County 911 Center, which handles more than one million emergency calls annually, was the first emergency center statewide to become an Accredited Center of Excellence, a prestigious national distinction, and in 2007 received a national award for intergovernmental cooperation.

Roughly 1.1 million people live in the Greater Rochester metropolitan area, which includes Genesee, Livingston, Monroe, Ontario, Orleans, Seneca, Wayne, Wyoming, and Yates counties. The city of Rochester occupies the northeast corner of Monroe County, where about two-thirds of the metro area's population resides.

Homes here are both affordable and architecturally striking. The median cost of a house in the Rochester region is only about half the national average: $121,800 compared to $224,900 elsewhere. The city comprises more than 35 neighborhoods, which formed in the late 19th and early 20th centuries as Rochester was becoming a thriving industrial destination and whose homes reflect the popular architectural styles of the period, including Queen Anne, Tudor revival, and American foursquare. The East Avenue corridor, with its large estates built for Rochester's earliest business elite, is one of the country's premier preservation districts. Historic suburban villages are anchored by charming, bustling commercial strips.

Monroe Avenue, an artery that connects downtown to several suburbs, is a shopper's paradise. The city's portion is lined on both sides with eclectic stores for every taste. The nearby communities of Brighton and Pittsford are known more for higher-end boutiques and upscale franchises.

Visual Impressions

Rochester has a multitude of cultural offerings, many of which have garnered attention both nationally and internationally. The George Eastman House International Museum of Photography and Film, named for the philanthropist known as the father of modern photography and inventor of motion picture film, houses the world's oldest photography museum and one of the world's oldest film archives. The museum, where North America's first school of film preservation was established, in 1997, is attached to the 50-room Colonial Revival mansion where Eastman lived.

With an international art collection spanning 5,000 years, the Memorial Art Gallery of the University of Rochester boasts 11,000 works and houses North America's only full-size Italian baroque organ. The Rochester Contemporary Art Center displays works by regional and national contemporary artists. Its smaller exhibition spaces showcase the work of local artists.

Opposite page, left: East Main Street near Chestnut Street in downtown Rochester; opposite page, right: A Corn Hill neighborhood home's architectural splendor.
This page: Patrons waiting to view "DARFUR/DARFUR," an exhibit at the George Eastman House International Museum of Photography and Film, 2007.

Stage and Screen

Cinematic and live theaters, many with in-house improvisational comedy troupes, showcase the classic and contemporary. Once offering lunchtime performances in the business school that originally housed it, Geva Theatre Center is now Rochester's leading professional playhouse and the state's most well-attended regional theater, drawing more than 174,000 patrons each year to performances on two stages in the historic Naval Armory building. The midsized professional Blackfriars Theatre, which produces six dramatic and musical plays a year, has been a stop for many artists who have moved on to acting and technical roles in theater, television, and movies. The Downstairs Cabaret Theatre, with an average annual attendance of 20,000, offers a rotation of musicals, comedies, and dramas on three stages.

The Little Theatre, which opened in October 1929 and is on the National Register of Historic Places, retains its original mission to serve as an alternative to the growing number of commercial movie houses by showcasing thought-provoking, cultural films. By 1996 the Little had expanded to include five screens and a 70-seat café featuring live jazz and a rotating exhibit of local artwork. The Dryden Theatre at the George Eastman House offers a smorgasbord of motion pictures, from silent and cult films to premieres of foreign and independent works. It attracts more than 40,000 filmgoers a year and has screened more than 13,000 titles using the original projectors installed when the theater was built in 1951.

The Rochester Philharmonic Orchestra demonstrates its musical versatility in ticketed and free performances, presenting more than 140 concerts a year attended by some 350,000 people. Founded by George Eastman in 1922, the innovative orchestra was the first in the country to create the position of Principal Conductor for Education and Outreach.

This page, top: A Mercury Opera Rochester presentation of *Amahl and the Night Visitors;* this page, bottom: A performance by members of Garth Fagan Dance. Opposite page: Dreyden Theatre at the George Eastman House.

Western New York's only professional opera company is Mercury Opera Rochester, which was incorporated in 2004 and generally offers up to four productions per season. Garth Fagan, the artist who created the groundbreaking, Tony Award–winning choreography for *The Lion King*, chose Rochester in 1970 as home base for Garth Fagan Dance, an internationally acclaimed company hailed for the originality of its choreography and the virtuosity of its dancers. Founded in 1987, the Rochester City Ballet regularly performs with world-renowned choreographers and has had many members advance to positions with the American Ballet Theatre, New York City Ballet, and other prestigious companies in both the United States and Europe.

A Legacy Remembered

Rochester's legacy of social activism is symbolized in a statue depicting two of its most famous residents, abolitionist and former slave Frederick Douglass and women's rights pioneer Susan B. Anthony. The statue, which shows the longtime friends sharing a cup of tea and conversation, is located in Susan B. Anthony Square, a small park a few blocks from Anthony's home, where she spent much of her time campaigning and hosting fellow reformers. Now a National Historic Landmark, the house is the site where Anthony was arrested in 1872, charged with voting illegally. Anthony is one of more than 200 inductees in the National Women's Hall of Fame in nearby Seneca Falls. The town, called "the Birthplace of Women's Rights," was the location of the first

women's rights convention, in 1848. Douglass is remembered at the Frederick Douglass Resource Center, under construction in the city's Susan B. Anthony neighborhood. A joint effort of the state, city, and the Frederick Douglass Community Development Corporation, it will include an exhibit hall, multipurpose theater, library, classrooms, and meeting rooms. Both Douglass and Anthony are honored in the newest addition to the city skyline, the Frederick Douglass–Susan B. Anthony Memorial Bridge. The award-winning project is said to be the widest triple-member arch bridge in the country.

Southwest of Rochester in Mumford, the Genesee Country Village and Museum is the largest living-history museum in New York and one of the largest in the nation. It showcases life in the 1800s as well as North America's premier collection of wildlife and sporting art.

Barbie and the Etch A Sketch are part of the world's largest and most comprehensive collection of toys and dolls found at the Strong National Museum of Play, home to the National Toy Hall of Fame, the Dancing Wings Butterfly Garden, Sesame Street, and other adventures. The Rochester Museum and Science Center offers three floors of hands-on, interactive exhibits on the region's contributions to the sciences, technology, and cultural diversity, as well as a planetarium presenting giant-screen films and rock-music laser light shows.

For the literary set, Writers and Books involves more than 25,000 area residents each year with readings, lectures, classes, discussion groups, and two annual communitywide book clubs. The center had been a mobile bookstore and distributor throughout the Northeast, playing a pivotal role in the rise of independent publishers, before putting down roots in Rochester in 1980.

Parks, Flowers, and Festivals

Monroe County's 12,000-acre, 21-park system originated in 1888, when nurserymen George Ellwanger and Patrick Barry donated 20 acres of gently sloping hills for a city park. The parcel, considered one of the country's first municipal arboretums, is now the center of Highland Park, one of several parks in Rochester designed by noted landscape architect Frederick Law Olmsted. The man behind New York City's Central Park, Olmsted also designed Rochester's Maplewood, Seneca, and Genesee Valley parks along the Genesee River.

Highland Park heralds warm weather's arrival each May with the Lilac Festival, drawing visitors from every continent to admire a collection of more than 1,200 lilac bushes that began with 20 varieties planted in 1892. This Rochester tradition unofficially kicks off the start of festival season—there are several festivals throughout the region every weekend during the summer alone.

Opposite page: The bronze sculpture *Let's Have Tea* by Pepsy Kettavong depicting Susan B. Anthony and Frederick Douglass in Susan B. Anthony Square.
This page: A family enjoying the annual Lilac Festival, a Rochester tradition since 1898.

Rochester is known for its wide array of popular festivals. The Clothesline Festival, one of many dedicated to arts and crafts, started more than 50 years ago and is a fund-raiser for the Memorial Art Gallery of the University of Rochester. The Rochester International Jazz Festival, established in 2002, is one of the country's largest and fastest-growing music festivals. It drew more than 600 artists from 15 countries in June 2007, with attendance jumping 51 percent over the previous year to 121,000. For 2008, almost 250 concerts were held at 15 venues over nine days. The Corn Hill Festival attracts more than 250,000 people a year. Rochester also has the Park Avenue Festival, the Puerto Rican Festival, the High Falls Film Festival, and many more events.

Unique Destinations

The Seneca Park Zoo opened in 1893 and in recent years has invested heavily in improvements, including a \$2.3 million Animal Health and Education Complex and a \$4.4 million African elephant exhibit. The Seabreeze Amusement Park, with more than 70 attractions, opened in 1879 and is the fourth-oldest continuously operating amusement park in North America.

Reigning as the country's oldest continuously operating farmers' market is the City of Rochester's Public Market, dating to 1827; it has been at its current nine-acre location since 1905. Shoppers can find everything from food and flowers to crafts and clothing, as well as attend events such as free summer concerts.

Given its varied topography and famous residents, the historic Mount Hope Cemetery is a destination for exercisers and tour groups. In addition to Susan B. Anthony and Frederick Douglass, notables laid to rest at the nation's first municipal Victorian cemetery include automobile inventor George B. Selden, newspaper publisher Frank E. Gannett, and many others.

On the Water

Set between Lake Ontario and the Erie Canal and with several waterfalls dotting the downtown along the Genesee River, Rochester once generated enough power to become the largest flour-producing city in North America. Although that industry has waned, the Brown's Race Historic District preserves its role with a museum and walking tours that lead to a panoramic view of the 96-foot High Falls and Genesee River Gorge.

The Port of Rochester, where the Genesee River flows into Lake Ontario, is undergoing major renovations as city officials develop the area into an urban village for residents, businesses, and tourists. The area abuts Ontario Beach Park, site of the annual Rochester Harbor and Carousel Festival. The port is the site of several major development projects planned or in the works to grow the area economy.

4PM-6PM
MON-FRI
ALEXANDER

FRESH FRUIT
AND VEGETABLES
MUTSU
(CRISPIN)
2.00
Yakov.
FAMILY FARM
Sodus, New York

A short drive from Rochester lies the stunning Finger Lakes region, a string of scenic waterways that draw more than one million tourists each year. Iroquois legend holds that the hand of the Great Spirit created the lakes as a reward for the Iroquois Confederacy's courage and devotion. Geologists cite the origin of the lakes as receding glaciers.

The region is one of the state's most important agricultural contributors, with some of the country's largest producers of milk, apples, grapes, and pumpkins. Perhaps more widely known as wine country, the region has more than 100 wineries that produce more than 100 million bottles of wine annually—making the Finger Lakes the country's largest wine-producing region outside California.

The New York Wine & Culinary Center in Canandaigua opened in 2006 to celebrate the area's achievements in the wine and food industries.

Rochester's four distinct seasons create year-round opportunities to appreciate the local landscape. Hundreds of miles of trails meander along the waters of Lake Ontario and the Erie Canal, in the woodlands that line the Genesee River Gorge, and through some 70 neighborhoods. Demonstrating their hardiness and good nature, residents compete in an annual upstate snow derby—the winner is the city that records the most snowfall—and participate in Coldrush, a city-sponsored string of indoor and outdoor events to celebrate the coldest months of the year.

Opposite page, left: A vineyard in the Finger Lakes region overlooking Keuka Lake; opposite page, right, and this page, left: The New York Wine & Culinary Center in Canandaigua. This page, right : A bicyclist on a path near the confluence of the Genesee River and the Erie Canal.

This page, left: Tommy Watkins at bat for the Rochester Red Wings; this page, left, and opposite page: The Rochester Americans hockey team battling on the ice.

City at Play

Sports fans have many teams to cheer in Rochester. The Red Wings baseball team, the Triple-A affiliate of the Minnesota Twins major-league club, is the oldest minor-league franchise in the history of professional sports, dating back to 1899. The Rochester Americans—known locally as the Amerks—joined the American Hockey League in 1956. They play at the 12,000-seat Blue Cross Arena at the War Memorial, a downtown landmark. Rochester is also home to the RazorSharks basketball team, Rhinos soccer team, Knighthawks indoor lacrosse team, Rattlers outdoor lacrosse team, and Raiders arena football team.

For outdoor football action, fans can observe the National Football League's Buffalo Bills summertime training camp at St. John Fisher College, which has hosted the camp since 2000. Admission is free to the daily practices, which attract fans from several states and Canada.

With more than 60 public and semiprivate courses and more than 20 private courses, the Rochester area is a golf destination. Locust Hill Country Club in Pittsford has hosted the Wegmans Rochester Ladies Professional Golf Association (LPGA) tournament for more than 30 years. Nearby Oak Hill Country Club has hosted two Professional Golfers' Association (PGA) Championships, a Senior PGA Championship, the Ryder Cup, two U.S. Amateur Championships, and three U.S. Opens.

Easy Access

Rochester's proximity to Interstates 390, 490, and 590 makes commuting relatively easy; the typical commute time is 20 minutes. The city is only minutes from the New York State Thruway with connections to 12 northeastern states within a 400-mile radius and to two of Canada's largest cities, Toronto and Montreal.

Public transportation is efficient and affordable. The Rochester Genesee Regional Transportation Authority transports 50,000 bus riders a day throughout seven counties. For air connections, the Greater Rochester International Airport has some 220 flights every day.

A Great City for Business

Despite being hit hard by major corporate layoffs, Rochester has more jobs today than it did in 1980. In fact, job growth is at three times the growth of population, in part because of help from networking and economic development organizations such as Greater Rochester Enterprise and the Rochester Business Alliance. In November 2007, Greater Rochester Enterprise launched an online service to show senior business executives, site selectors, and corporate real estate brokers the advantages of setting up shop in the region.

Local companies also benefit by taking advantage of various tax credits from the New York State Empire Zone program, which offers some of the best business-incentive packages in the United States. The support undoubtedly contributes to the area's having the country's highest number of patents per worker, a feat that earned it kudos from *Forbes* as "First in Innovation."

Also helping bring business to the area is VisitRochester, Monroe County's official tourism promotion agency, which develops meeting and convention business and markets the area as a vacation destination. The busy Rochester Riverside Convention Center draws a high volume of visitors for conventions, trade shows, public shows, corporate meetings, galas, and other events.

Rochester has much to offer. It is a city of opportunity, where innovation brings success. It is also a city of promise, where a vibrant lifestyle, including unique cultural and recreational offerings, makes people proud to call the city home.

Opposite page, top: Java's, a downtown coffeehouse; opposite page, bottom: One of the Rochester Genesee Regional Transportation Authority's many convenient buses. This page: The Wilder Building, right, at the Four Corners area at West Main and State streets.

This page: Magnetic resonance imaging (MRI) scans in color, which provide more efficient diagnoses. Opposite page: An optics professional checking a lens.

CHAPTERTWO

Biotechnology, Life Sciences, and Optics

WORLD-CLASS RESEARCH

Rochester and the surrounding nine counties—long known for an entrepreneurial spirit, innovation, and biomedical breakthroughs—are home to more than 70 industry-related companies that employ more than 8,000 people. Between five and 15 new ventures are launched each year, many specializing in vision science and medical imaging. Those numbers are expected to grow as tech incubators continue to arise, nurturing new companies hoping to transition from research and development to commercial success.

Growing New Technologies

The 40,000-square-foot Rochester BioVenture Center opened in Henrietta in July 2007. Launched by the University of Rochester Medical Center and managed by High Tech Rochester (HTR), a not-for-profit economic development organization, it is supported by $2.5 million in state funding and provides mentoring and wet lab facilities for up to a dozen fledgling businesses that plan to move out on their own after three to five years. Tenants include Egenix, which develops cancer therapeutics, and NaturalNano, which finds new ways to use materials such as industrial polymers and plastics.

Young companies also seek guidance at HTR's Lennox Tech Enterprise Center and the Rochester Institute of Technology's High Technology Incubator, both in Henrietta, and the Infotonics Technology Center in Canandaigua.

Local biotech giants include Genencor International, UCB (formerly Celltech Pharmaceuticals), and Biophan Technologies. Ortho-Clinical Diagnostics in the nearby town of Greece, now a subsidiary of Johnson & Johnson, has become a leader in diagnosing diseases with a technology that harkens back to its days as Johnson and Johnson Clinical Diagnostics, once a division of Eastman Kodak—a company with ties to many area start-ups. Headquartered in Raritan, New Jersey, Ortho-Clinical Diagnostics is committing $80 million to maintain and expand operations in the Rochester area, where its workforce totals more than 1,100 people. The company announced $1.4 billion in sales in 2006.

Unlike large, multimarket firms with blockbuster budgets, many start-ups focus on a niche, a strategy that economic development experts believe is necessary for biotech firms to succeed in a midsize market like Rochester. These same experts point to local success as a boon to the upstate economy's renaissance.

A History of Cutting-Edge Research

The region has a strong track record of turning out new technologies with commercial appeal. Rochester's relationship with translational research—the term applied to the journey from laboratory to clinical setting—can be traced back to University of Rochester School of Medicine and Dentistry founding dean George Hoyt Whipple. His research in the 1920s on the physiology of the liver eventually led to a treatment for pernicious anemia, for which he shared a Nobel Prize in 1934.

Most agree that the area's industry owes its beginnings to the $50 million (worth more than half a billion in today's market) that Eastman Kodak founder George Eastman gave the university in the 1920s and early 1930s. This initial funding paved the way for future generations of cutting-edge research and development.

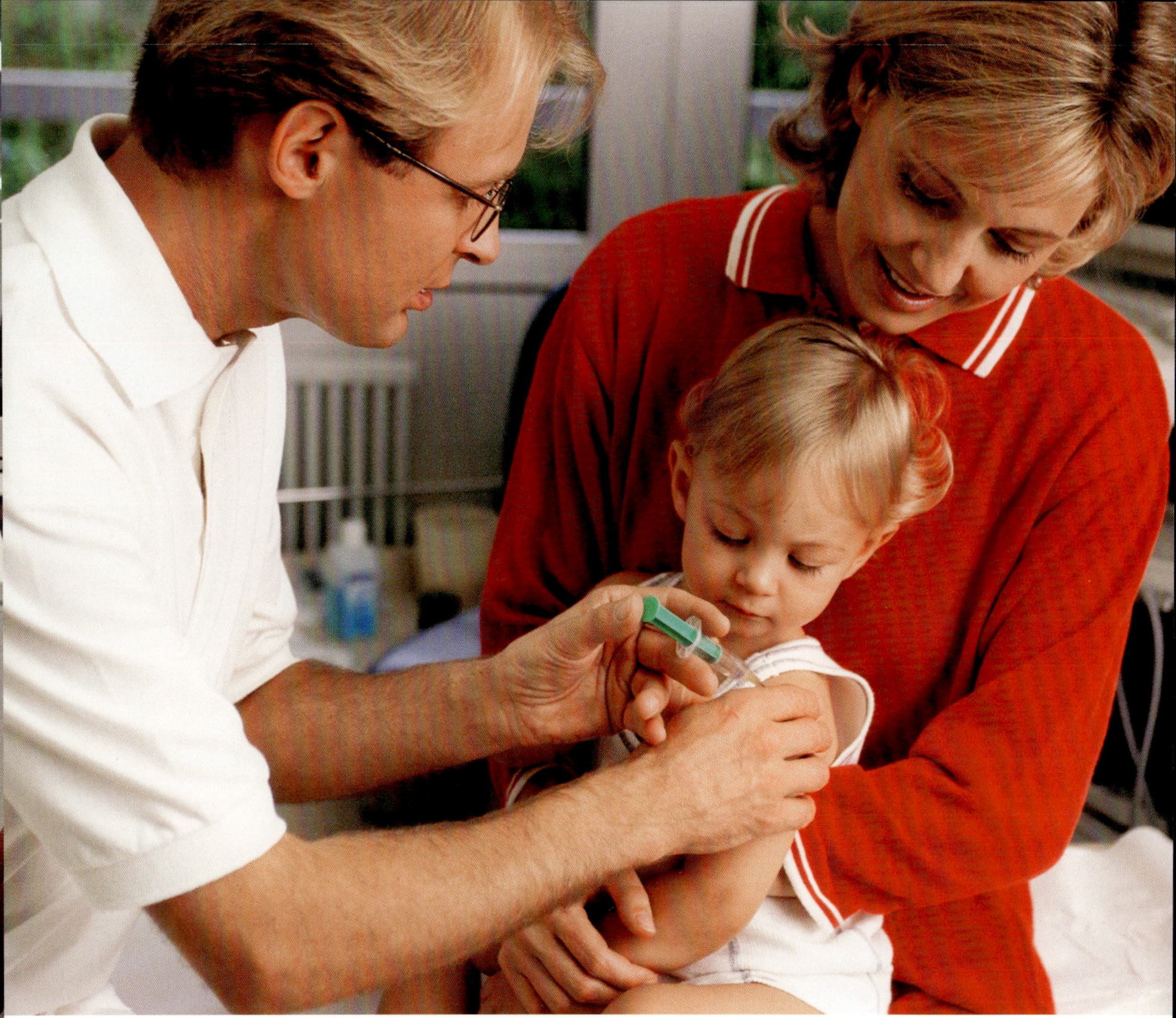

The University of Rochester Medical Center, which employs more than 14,700 people, is a national leader among biomedical research institutions. Its discoveries include the cox-2 enzyme, which spurred a new class of arthritis medications, including the well-known Celebrex, and the HiB vaccine against bacterial meningitis, which has become universally recommended for young children and is responsible for virtually eliminating the infection in the United States. In June 2007, after 20 years of research by three university virologists, the Food and Drug Administration approved a high-profile vaccine targeting certain strains of human papillomaviruses, which cause 12,000 cases of cervical cancer in the United States each year.

Opposite page: Employees of XLI Corporation, a precision manufacturing company that has worked with High Tech Rochester's Manufacturing Extension Partnership. This page, left: A laboratory technician preparing samples for cancer screening; this page, right: A child getting her HiB vaccination, a University of Rochester Medical Center discovery that protects against bacterial meningitis.

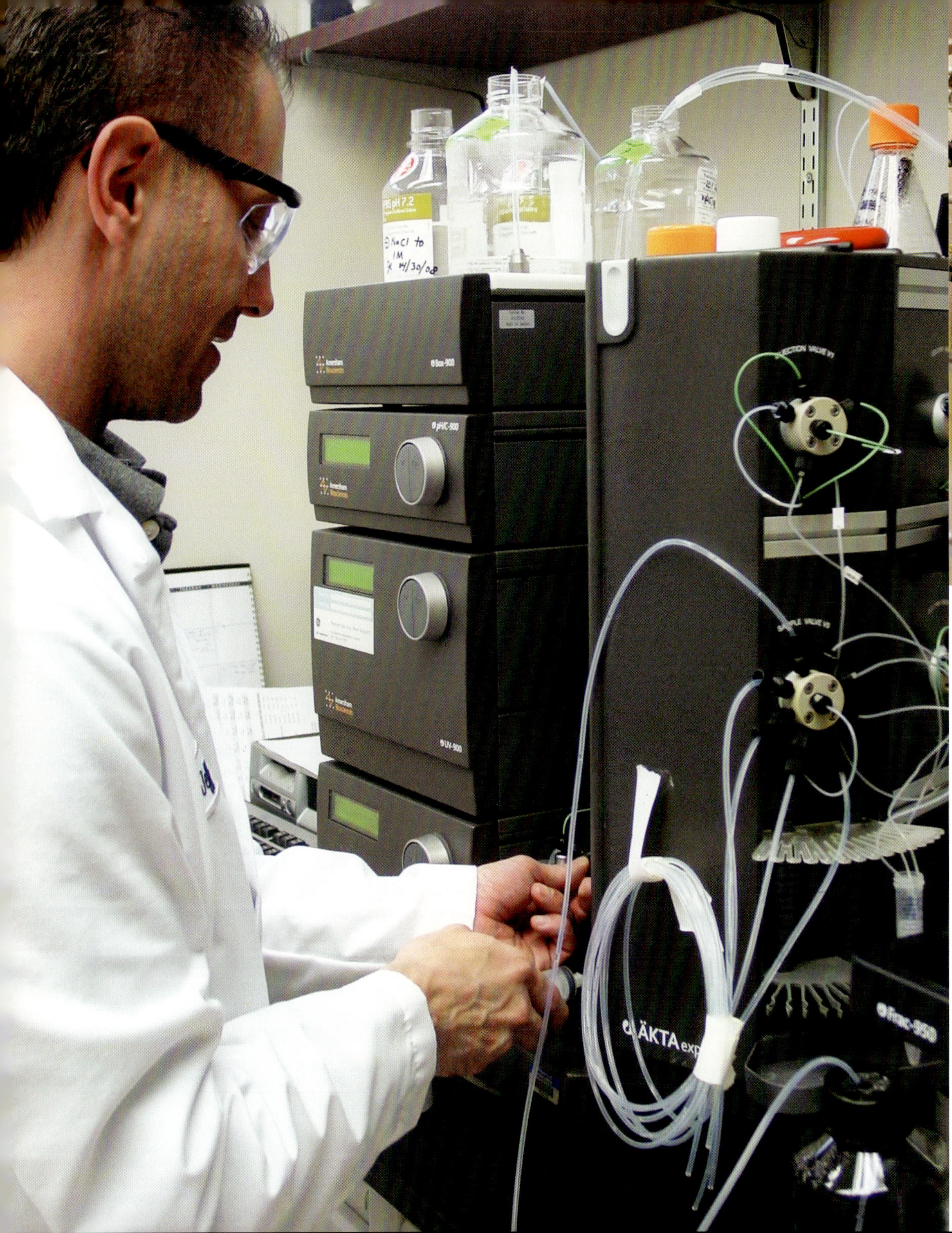

The University of Rochester has seen discoveries triple and patents double since 2000 and is among the nation's top 10 universities to earn royalty revenue from licensed intellectual property. Funding from the National Institutes of Health almost doubled from $72 million in 1995 to $142 million in 2006. Add in other funding sources, and the medical center overall receives more than $230 million a year for medical research. A Clinical and Translational Sciences Institute, scheduled to open in late 2009 as an effective conduit to commercialization, is expected to generate $30 million annually by its fifth year. New York State committed $50 million in 2008 to help make the institute a reality.

Roughly 30 start-ups have grown out of the university's research. Vaccinex, which has received more than $20 million in venture funding and $10 million in research grants, develops therapeutic antibodies to help pharmaceutical companies determine whether a drug is effective. VirtualScopics in Pittsford creates software that converts ordinary CT and MRI scans into three-dimensional color images, allowing analysts in pharmaceutical and medical-device clinical trials to more closely track the progress of various diseases. In Brighton, iCardiac Technologies develops products that let pharmaceutical companies determine earlier on in clinical trials whether an experimental drug is toxic to the heart.

Productive Partnerships

The Rochester region and the state show their commitment to turning discoveries into new companies by forging partnerships among businesses, universities, and government. The state-sponsored Center for Electronic Imaging Systems matches local researchers with biomedical imaging businesses across the state, from giants such as Bausch & Lomb and Eastman Kodak to smaller companies whose budgets may not be large enough to cover full-time scientists. The center reported a record economic impact of $120 million statewide during its 2006–07 fiscal year. Even greater results are forecast from a $2 million state grant, awarded in 2006 to help bring biomedical imaging technology to market. It is expected to net a regional economic impact of $200 million over four years.

The Rochester Institute of Technology (RIT), known for preparing students for emerging technical fields, led a collaboration with the University of Buffalo and Allegany County's Alfred University to share research on microsystems, photonics, remote sensing systems, and nanomaterials. The IT Collaboratory was built at RIT in 2001 with a $14 million grant from the New York State Office of Science, Technology, and Academic Research. Work there has led to more than $26 million in research grants, 27 invention disclosures, 18 patents issued or pending, and four start-up companies.

RIT earned its biotech bragging rights back in 1983 with the establishment of the country's first biotechnology baccalaureate program, one that remains a national model. The college launched a bioinformatics program in 2002.

This page: Bausch & Lomb world headquarters on the left, with the Xerox Tower on the right in downtown Rochester. Opposite page: The contact lens, a major product of Rochester's optical companies.

Collaborations also exist to ensure that the region's highly skilled, competitive workforce remains at the top of its game. After a yearlong study found that biotechnology companies across Western New York lacked training and professional development programs for employees, RIT opened the Center for Bioscience Education and Technology. The 35,000-square-foot, state-of-the-art building hosts, among other things, customized workshops, seminars, and training programs on a fee-for-service basis.

Along with Rochester's talent pool and central location, economic incentives and financing from Empire State Development and the County of Monroe Industrial Development Agency are major factors in a company's decision to move or expand here. Rochester Business Alliance, the regional chamber of commerce, and Greater Rochester Enterprise, a regional economic development organization, provide additional support.

Leading the Optics Industry

Headquartered in Rochester since its founding in 1853, eye care company Bausch & Lomb pioneered many developments in optics, including the first optical-quality glass made in the United States, glare-reducing sunglasses, and the first soft contact lens. What started long ago with a $60 loan and a handshake has blossomed into a global enterprise. The company showed its commitment to Rochester when it nearly doubled the size of its main research, development, and engineering center in December 2006. The $35 million project includes a 75,000-square-foot glass-and-brick wing filled with laboratories and offices, with room for a future 25,000-square-foot addition. Bausch & Lomb ended its tenure as a public company in October 2007 when the private equity firm Warburg Pincus, based in New York City, acquired the company for $4.5 billion. Bausch & Lomb employs approximately 13,000 people worldwide and 1,500 in Rochester.

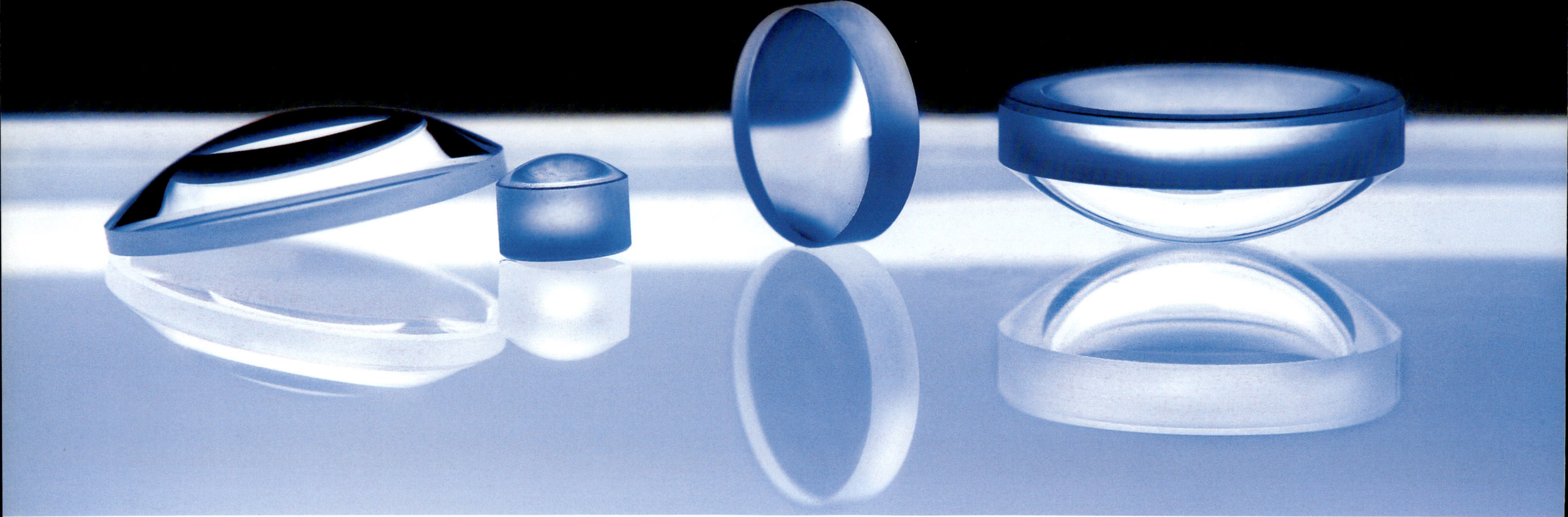

Carestream Health, a provider of dental and medical imaging products, agreed to retain headquarters and grow the company in Rochester after Onex Corporation of Toronto, Canada, bought the group from Kodak in 2007. Before Onex renamed it, it was the Kodak Health Group. The decision to stay in Rochester saved 800 jobs, including a pledge to add 500 more jobs over six years, and involved an investment of $12 million in building upgrades. With revenues of more than $2.5 billion, the company employs 1,400 people locally and about 8,100 globally. Its products are in 90 percent of hospitals and dental offices worldwide.

CooperVision, the world's third-largest contact lens manufacturer and the number-one maker of toric lenses, chose the region over a competing California location—hours from its headquarters in Orange County, California—to open a North American distribution center in Henrietta. The move created 225 jobs and retained more than 200 workers from its existing local distribution center in the Rochester area.

Rochester's leadership in the optics world includes several firsts. The Optical Society of America, a national optics and photonics trade association, was founded in Rochester in 1916. Today it has more than 14,000 members from 81 countries. The University of Rochester's Institute of Optics, the country's first higher-education program of its kind in the field, has awarded degrees to more than half the people working in the U.S. optics industry. In 1963 Monroe Community College became the first school in the country to offer a two-year degree for optics technicians.

Such history brings credibility and prestige to businesses in the region's growing optics, imaging, and photonics industry. After buying Kodak's precision glass manufacturing unit in 2005, Rochester Precision Optics renovated a Henrietta manufacturing plant instead of moving operations to New Hampshire, where the company is based.

Ninety percent of the companies in the New York Photonics Industry Association are based within 20 minutes of downtown Rochester. This Rochester Regional Photonics Cluster, with more than 100 members, is a collaborative group offering infrastructure and resources for a variety of industries, including aerospace, microelectronics, and telecommunications. Members range from established firms like Corning Tropel to small start-ups like Lumetrics, which employs 13 people and uses light to analyze the thickness of specialty film, flexible packaging, plastics, and other materials.

Rochester's accomplishments, expertise, and facilities make it a highly sought-after destination in biotechnology, life sciences, and optics.

Opposite page: Precision molded glass aspheric optics lenses made in Rochester, a center of the optics industry. This page: Reviewing medical scans on imaging systems from Carestream Health.

This page: An Eastman Kodak employee in Rochester inspecting a silicon wafer that holds printheads for Kodak ink-jet photo printers.
Opposite page: Pringles containers, with freshness assured by seals from American Packaging.

CHAPTER THREE

Manufacturing and Food Processing

REINVENTED FOR THE 21ST CENTURY

As home to Eastman Kodak, Xerox, and Bausch & Lomb, Rochester became widely known for its manufacturing muscle. Today the local manufacturing industry is reinventing itself, as niche markets absorb the sector's job losses and traditional methods give way to high-tech, high-profile products—an economic trend that has county officials boasting that jobs are growing at three times the rate of population growth. The area's abundant combination of fertile soil and freshwater, meanwhile, is responsible for one of the largest wine- and dairy-producing regions in the country. More than 100 food and beverage manufacturing companies have set up operations here.

The Big Three

Eastman Kodak, Xerox, and Bausch & Lomb, long ago nicknamed "the Big Three," each retain a powerful influence in the region's evolving manufacturing market. Kodak, founded in 1888 by George Eastman, now focuses on digital imaging for use in entertainment and film, graphic communications, commercial printing, and consumer products, including ways for people to view and share pictures. Its online EasyShare Gallery has more than 60 million registered members and two billion stored photos. With 12,500 of its 40,000 employees in Rochester, Kodak reported $10.3 billion in sales in 2007.

Xerox, which specializes in document management, began in Rochester and moved its headquarters in 1969 to Connecticut. The company does research, manufacturing, engineering, assembling, marketing, and sales at its Rochester operations, and has additional facilities in nearby Webster, New York. It is the Rochester region's fourth-largest employer, with more than 7,000 workers.

Bausch & Lomb has grown from a small downtown optical shop in the mid 1850s into a global leader in eye health. It continually sends to market innovative optical designs for a variety of sight conditions and lighting situations. Its products, available in more than 100 countries, include various types of contact lenses and ReNu, the nation's top-selling contact lens solution. The company also makes products and systems for eye surgery.

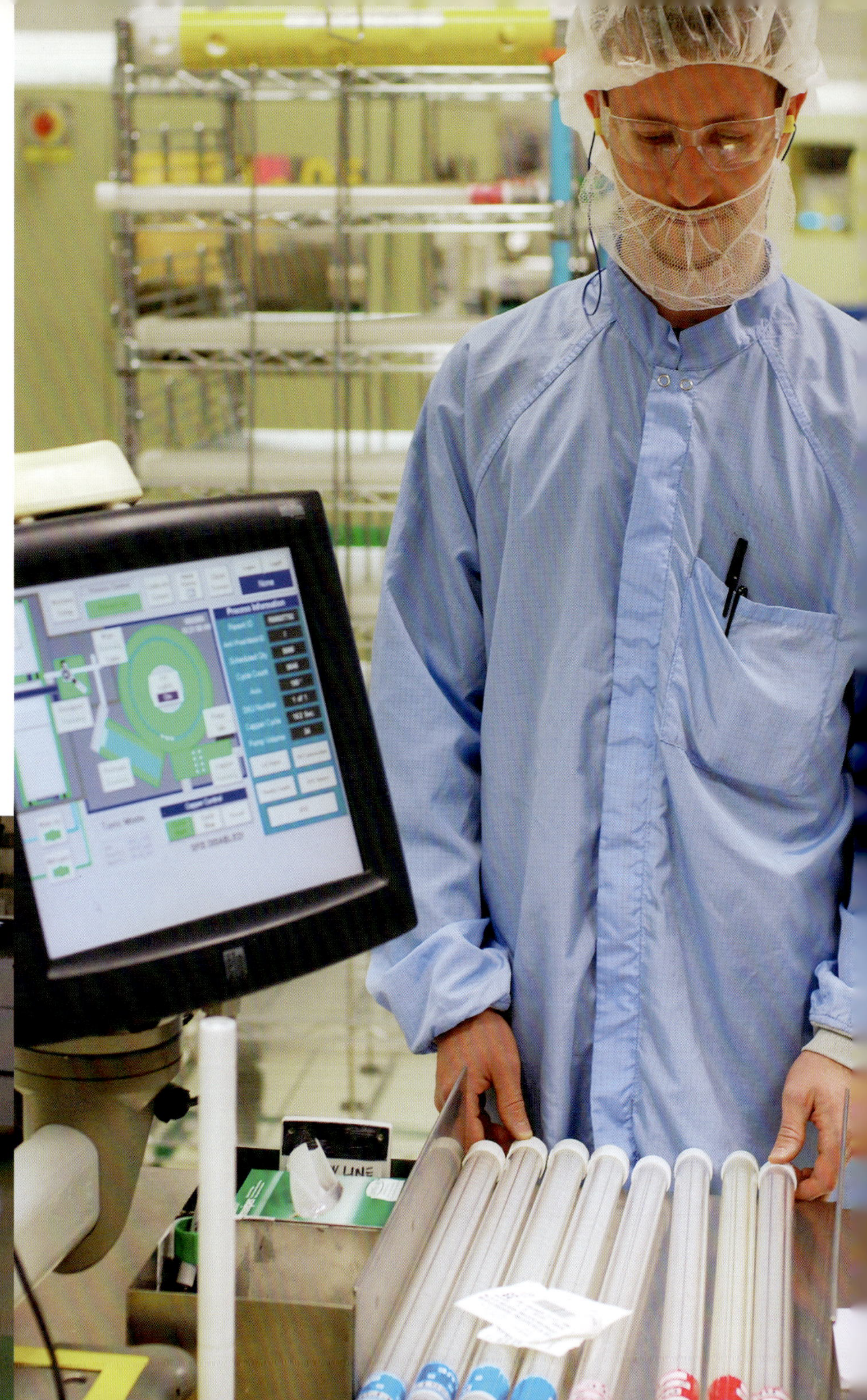

Packaging Redesigned

Packaging companies play a significant role in Rochester, producing functional products for numerous national brands and inventing new designs that take convenience to the next level. Pactiv Corporation developed the OneZip and Cinch Sak bags for its Hefty brand at its Canandaigua plant, southeast of Rochester, one of 39 Pactiv plants across North America. The company, which makes specialty packaging for consumers and various food-service industries, has pledged to invest $73 million to expand operations, which would put the number of local employees near 1,100. The expansion of the facility and the addition of jobs would make Pactiv eligible to apply for various economic benefits.

At its two manufacturing plants in Henrietta, south of Rochester, Diamond Packaging produces nearly 400 million folding cartons, cards, and inserts a year for companies such as Procter and Gamble, Godiva, and L'Oréal. ExxonMobil Chemical in Wayne County develops and tests the plastic wrappers used for Hershey bars. From American Packaging of Rochester come sealed tops for Pringles potato chip cans and lids for single-serving sizes of Lipton soups and Wheaties cereal. The company also tests bags of lettuce for Dole Food.

Part of Thermo-Fisher Scientific, Nalgene Flexible Products makes child-resistant, reclosable, stand-up pouches that hold such things as medicine for the pharmaceutical industry and chemical protection suits for the military.

Opposite page, left: A commercial printer perusing a book digitally printed and bound on advanced book-publishing equipment from Xerox; opposite page, right: An employee on the contact lens manufacturing floor at the Bausch & Lomb Optics Center. This page, left; A Hefty OneZip bag from Pactiv; this page,

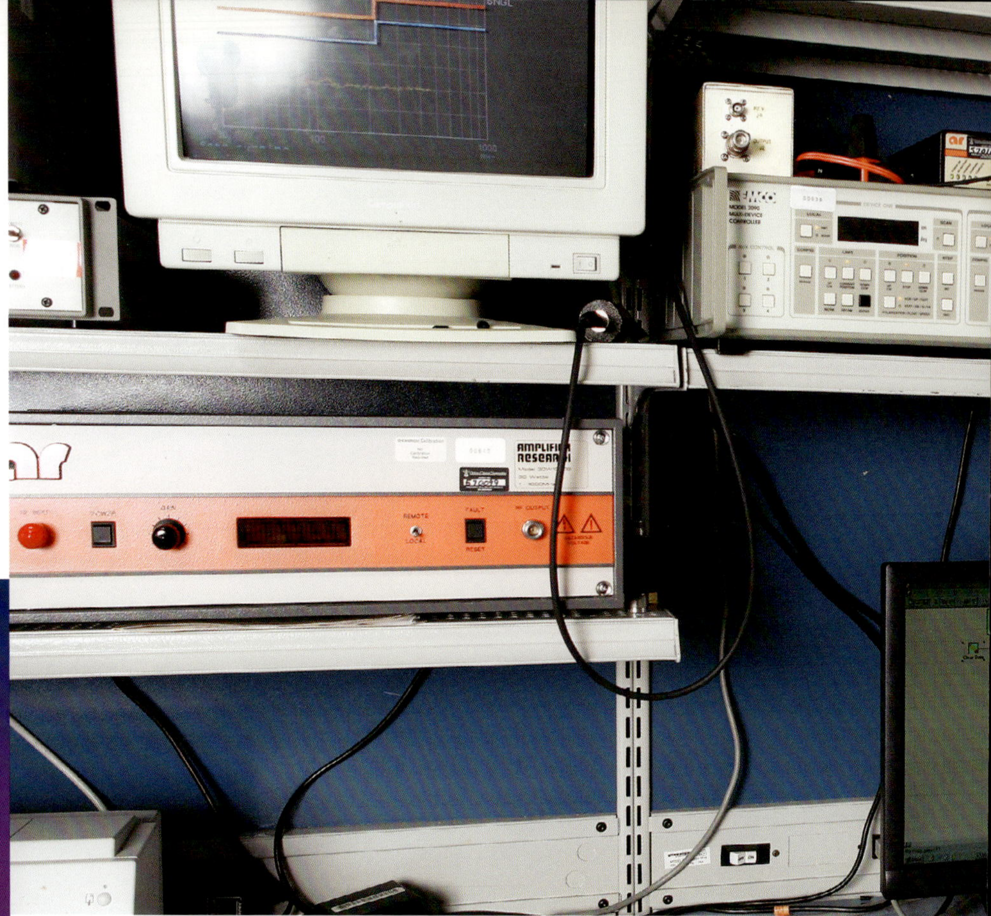

Geared for Global Success

With the presence of automobile-parts manufacturer Delphi, which has more than 1,500 local employees, the Rochester area is also a major player in the production of parts and components. Animatics Corp. manufactures motion-control devices for the semiconductor, nuclear, automotive, and machine tool industries. The fast-growing Silicon Valley company invested $700,000 to establish an East Coast presence in Rochester in 2007, giving a high-tech makeover to a century-old, former cigar manufacturing plant in the inner city.

Gleason Corporation began in 1865 as a Rochester machine shop started by William Gleason, inventor of the first bevel gear planer. It is now a world leader in the manufacture of equipment that is used to make bevel and cylindrical gears for everything from power tools to wind turbines. By focusing on highly productive advanced technology, the company has doubled its worldwide sales in recent years. Gleason employs about 700 people in Rochester, one of nine manufacturing sites across the globe.

Parker Hannifin, which dates to 1918, provides motion and control technologies and systems for commercial, mobile, industrial, and aerospace markets. It made the fuel and hydraulic-flow systems for the pioneering Boeing 787 Dreamliner, which had its first test flight in 2007. Its manufacturing plants in the Rochester area contribute to the company's 3,200 product lines and to its place among the top five longest-running, dividend-increase record-holders in the S&P 500 index. Sales reached $9.4 billion in 2006.

This page, left: A SmartMotor integrated motion-control system from Animatics; this page, right, and opposite page, left: A member of the Test Services group of Webster Plastics, part of the Chomerics division of Parker Hannifin, monitoring a client's electronics for verification and certification. Opposite page, right: A sergeant in the U.S. Army serving in Iraq with a tactical radio from Harris RF Communications Division, a world leader in secure voice and data communications systems.

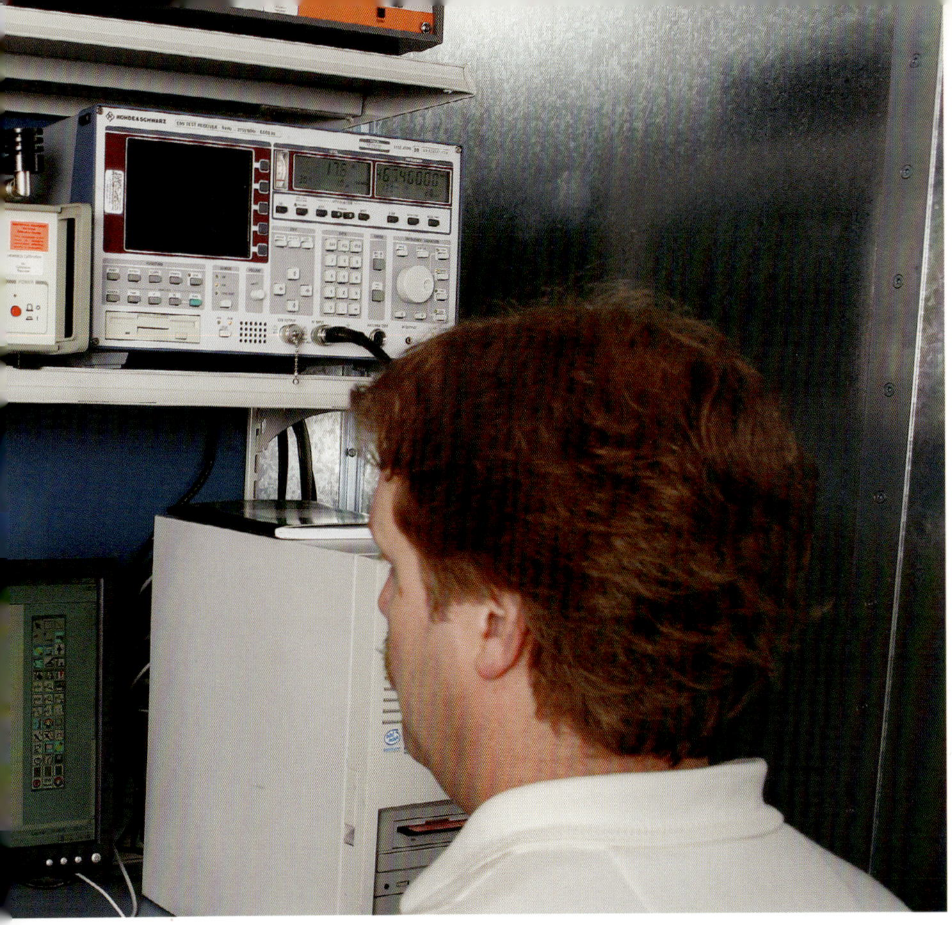

Nukote International has earned worldwide standing as a leader in imaging supplies, providing products such as ink-jet and toner cartridges for more than 30,000 imaging devices. Since relocating its corporate headquarters to Rochester in 2006, Nukote has hired administrative staff and established a regional distribution facility. It plans to add another 40 employees by mid 2008 and invest up to $10 million in new product development over three years.

Advanced Communications Technology

Given the number of local educational institutions producing highly qualified engineers, Rochester has a particular appeal to communications equipment manufacturers and is becoming a recognized leader in the field of remote sensing. Harris RF Communications Division in Rochester produces tactical radios and other communications equipment used by fighting and peace-keeping forces worldwide. Part of Harris Corporation, which is headquartered in Melbourne, Florida, the division has 2,200 employees in Rochester.

Alstom Signaling produces railway signal switches and relays. It is a division of Alstom, a global leader in power generation and rail transport. Its West Henrietta operation has secured 2,400 patents since 1904. Alstom, which has locations in more than 70 countries, had annual revenues of more than $20 billion during the 2006-07 fiscal year.

The View from on High

A number of area companies contribute to the defense, intelligence, and aerospace industries. One is ITT Space Systems Division, headquartered in Rochester and formed in 2004 after ITT bought Kodak's Remote Sensing Systems division. The company, with 1,800 workers in Monroe County, is helping to develop the James Webb Space Telescope, the successor to the Hubble Telescope.

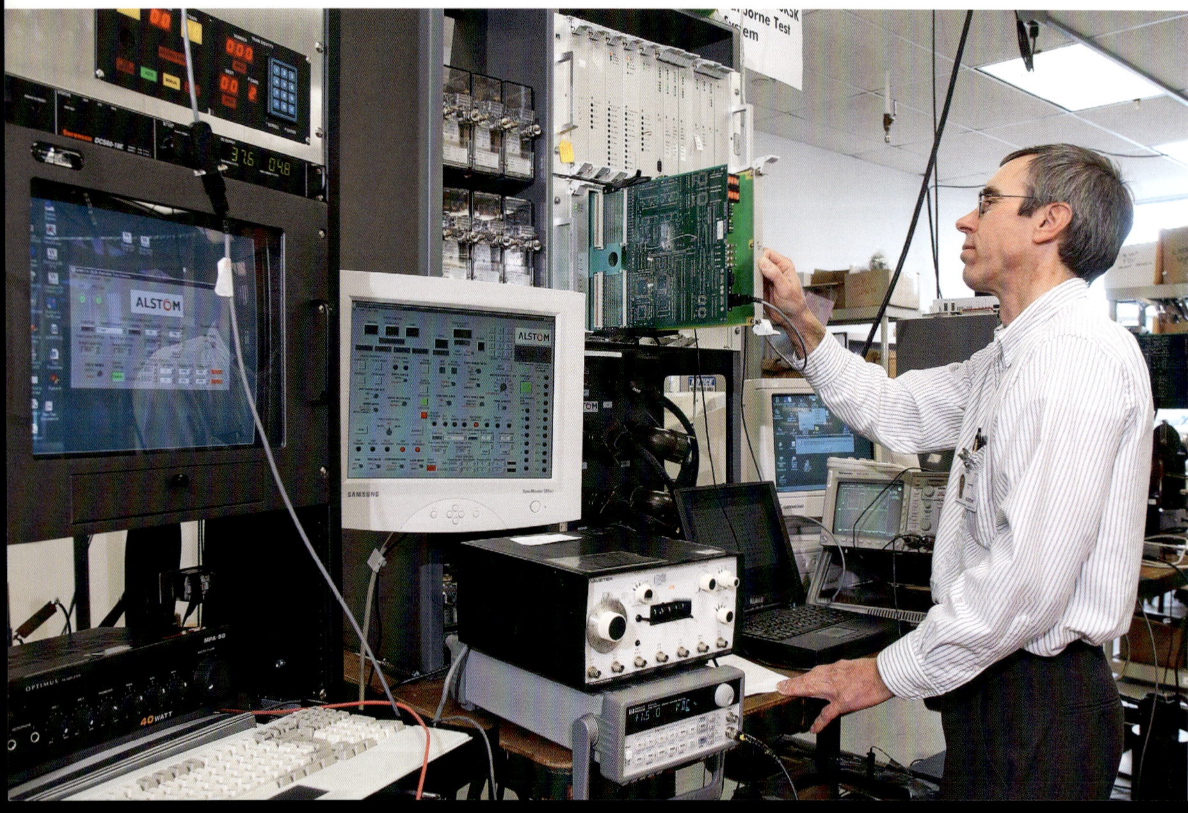

Wayne County's Optimax Systems is also getting otherworldly exposure, with NASA using its specialized lenses for missions to Mars and Pluto. Laser modules made at LaserMax in Henrietta have flown on several U.S. Space Shuttle missions; the company's laser accessories for firearms are used regularly by police and the military.

Pictometry International, a fast-growing start-up in Henrietta, has revolutionized aerial photography. Its visual information systems capture detailed images digitally and at various angles to help public safety agencies, first responders, and others do their jobs more quickly and accurately. Clients include Microsoft and Blom ASA of Norway, which is using Pictometry technology over 10 years to digitally photograph 13 European countries.

A Toast to Rochester

Besides holding the title as the largest milk-producing region in the state and the third-largest nationwide, the Rochester area is home to the world's largest wine producer. Once a small winery in the Finger Lakes town of Canandaigua, Constellation Brands in Fairport produced approximately 110 million cases in some 60 facilities in 2006, the equivalent of 1.3 billion 750-milliliter bottles of wine. The company markets and sells more than 250 brands of wine, imported beers, and spirits in approximately 150 countries and generates annual net sales topping $5 billion.

The 45-acre, Mediterranean-style Casa Larga Vineyards, also in Fairport, opened in 1974 and remains Monroe County's only winery, producing 24 different varieties.

Named after the scenic Genesee River waterfall it overlooks, High Falls Brewing Company is one of the oldest and largest continually operating breweries in the United States. The former Genesee Brewing Company brews and distributes a variety of beers, energy drinks, and other malt-based beverages.

The award-winning Custom BrewCrafters creates more than 50 unique brews for restaurants and taverns across Western New York. Located in the quaint village of Honeoye Falls, the brewery offers tours to the public and tastings of popular and seasonal selections. The Rohrbach Brewing Company has a microbrewery and restaurant that offer monthly food-and-beer pairings. Its award-winning lagers and ales are served at more than 100 upstate locations. Rohrback recently relocated its brewery to larger quarters on Railroad Street.

Opposite page, left: An array of signal and switching equipment at Alstom Signaling; opposite page, right, and this page, left: A digital aerial view of Rochester's Oak Hill Country Club from Pictometry International. This page, right: A worker at a labeling machine at the Centerra Wine Company, part of Constellation Brands, the world's largest wine producer.

This page: Members of the Wegman family—Danny, Colleen, and Nicole (behind Danny)—congratulating the bakery staff at a Wegmans Food Market.
Opposite page: Rotini boxes coming off the line at the Barilla America plant near Rochester.

Setting Supermarket Standards

Wegmans Food Markets, a Rochester-based supermarket chain that started in the early 1900s as a push-cart operation, now operates more than 70 stores in five states. Wegmans builds stores as large as 130,000 square feet featuring amenities that include baked goods, seafood, international foods, gourmet ready-to-eat entrees, and much more. Still family-owned, the gastronomic trendsetter has been recognized as one of *Fortune* magazine's 100 Best Companies to Work For since 1998. Wegmans captured the number one spot in 2005, the number two spot in 2006, and number three in 2007. With tax breaks from the County of Monroe Industrial Development Agency, Wegmans is building a $22 million Culinary Innovation Center in the Town of Chili for developing new products and manufacturing soups, sauces, and marinades.

Tops Friendly Markets is another major grocery retailer, with more than 70 full-service supermarkets in Western and Central New York and northern Pennsylvania. Its origins trace back to Niagara Falls in the early 1900s.

Filling the Shelves

Some of the most recognizable names in the food industry have operations in the region, including Seneca Foods, whose canned vegetables can be found in one of every three cupboards in America, and Birds Eye Foods, the country's top producer of frozen vegetables. Other well-known food brands produced or processed in the Rochester region include Kraft, Frito-Lay, Mott's, Heluva Good, Pepsi Bottling Group, and LiDestri, which packages Newman's Own sauces.

Saying they wanted to invest in a region that felt like home, officials with Barilla America, the world's largest pasta maker, based in Parma, Italy, are investing $96.2 million in a pasta production and distribution facility in Livingston County. The plant opened in 2007; once it reaches full capacity in 2009, it will produce 100,000 tons of pasta annually.

Rochester today is a leader in advanced manufacturing and food and beverage production. The region's engineering expertise and business acumen help companies thrive through innovative product development and efficient operations.

This page: Graduates gazing at the tower of Rush Reese Library on the University of Rochester campus on commencement day. Opposite page: One of the nearly 72,000 people employed in the region's health care and social services industries.

CHAPTER FOUR

Education and Health Care

OUTSTANDING INSTITUTIONS

Education and health care are vital to a community, and Rochester often is cited nationally for its solid standing in both areas. The metropolitan region claims 14 colleges and universities and seven community colleges or two-year career institutions serving more than 80,000 students a year. In health care, Rochester continues to set standards at its hospitals by offering cutting-edge procedures, expanding emergency rooms, and conducting legions of clinical trials that consistently change the way people live.

A Tradition of Excellence

Founded in 1850, the University of Rochester is one of the country's top private universities but small in size, with a little more than 4,600 undergraduates. Degrees are offered at the bachelor's, master's, and doctoral levels in six colleges or schools, including the world-renowned William E. Simon Graduate School of Business Administration and the School of Nursing, which recently underwent an $8.1 million expansion and renovation.

The University of Rochester owes a great debt of gratitude to Kodak magnate George Eastman, who made the school his primary beneficiary by giving it about half of his fortune. As a result, the University of Rochester is home to, among other namesakes, the Eastman School of Music, one of the world's most prestigious music conservatories. The school reviews more than 2,000 applications each year to accept approximately 260 new students, some 25 percent of whom arrive from foreign countries. Innovative programs complement traditional music training to help the school's 900 students blend their talents with the demands of today's job market.

A Leader in Technology

The heritage of the Rochester Institute of Technology (RIT) dates back to 1829, when Colonel Nathaniel Rochester and other community leaders founded the Athenaeum, a popular cultural center focusing on literature, science, and the arts. In 1885 Henry Lomb and other business leaders founded the Mechanics Institute to provide technical training. The institutions merged in 1891. In 1944 the institute adopted the current name. RIT now enrolls more than 15,000 students in professional and career programs. Its cooperative education program is one of the oldest and largest in the country, each year matching roughly 3,500 students with nearly 2,000 businesses.

Since opening its doors in September 1968, RIT's National Technical Institute for the Deaf (NTID) has been an international model for educating deaf and hard-of-hearing students for technical and business careers. RIT was chosen over eight other colleges to become home to the NTID, which serves as a resource for educators from as far away as Japan and the Philippines.

Knowledge for the Future

Rochester's liberal arts colleges provide students with the broad-ranging skills necessary for today's ever-changing workplace. Nazareth College, founded in 1924, is an independent institution set on 150 picturesque acres in Pittsford. With more than 3,000 students, the college has a student-faculty ratio of 12 to one and balances academic education with an emphasis on community service.

Also in Pittsford, St. John Fisher College was founded in 1948 as a Catholic college for men by the Congregation of St. Basil. It became independent in 1968 and began admitting women in 1971. The private college, with more than 3,000 students on its 154-acre campus, offers 31 majors and 13 graduate programs in five schools.

Four nearby schools are part of the 64-campus State University of New York (SUNY) system. The College at Brockport, State University of New York, set in a small town on the historic Erie Canal, has more than 8,000 students enrolled in 47 undergraduate programs, 29 graduate programs, and 23 areas of teacher certification. It is the region's largest public graduate school. The college, which began in 1835 as the Brockport Collegiate Institute, was a founding member of SUNY when the state university system was established in 1948. Its spacious, wooded campus features many modern amenities, including a new $18 million town home residence complex.

Opposite page, left: Rehearsal at the Eastman School of Music, University of Rochester; opposite page, right: Biology class at the Rochester Institute of Technology's National Technical Institute for the Deaf. This page: Performance by the Sankofa African Dance and Drum Ensemble of The College at Brockport, State University of New York.

Just 30 minutes south of Rochester is SUNY Geneseo, which opened as a teacher-training school in 1871 and became part of the SUNY system in 1948. SUNY Geneseo offers 54 degree programs to some 5,600 students. SUNY Empire State College in Irondequoit offers a flexible schedule for adult learners, with online and weekend classes.

Monroe Community College (MCC), also part of the SUNY system, serves some 36,000 students at a number of sites and is a member of the prestigious international organization the League for Innovation in the Community College. MCC dates back to the early 1960s, when local doctor Samuel J. Stabins rallied community leaders to establish the school in an effort to increase the workforce in area hospitals and health care offices. MCC offers 85 degree and certificate programs in career and occupational training in technical, health care, education, public safety, agriculture, and other fields. Many of these programs allow students to transfer to four-year colleges.

Religious Connections

The area's religious colleges have deep historical roots. In North Chili, Roberts Wesleyan College has been turning out thoughtful graduates prepared to transform society since 1866—when it was founded as Chili Seminary by

B. T. Roberts, the first bishop of a new denomination known as the Free Methodist Church. The college serves more than 1,800 students.

Colgate Rochester Crozer Divinity School has expanded from its Baptist roots into an ecumenical community. Its influential alumni include Pledge of Allegiance author Francis Bellamy and Marjorie Matthews, the first woman to be elected bishop in the United Methodist Church. St. Bernard's School of Theology and Ministry opened as a Roman Catholic seminary in 1893; since 1981 it has offered programs in theological and ministerial studies to address contemporary issues of the church and society.

This page: The Laboratory for Laser Energetics at the University of Rochester Medical Center, where experiments in implosion and basic physics are conducted, among other activities. Opposite page: A patient who received a defibrilator at Strong Memorial Hospital consulting with a nurse practioner.

An Emphasis on Health Care

The Rochester area has exceptional health care offerings, including teaching and research hospitals. Comprehensive programs are available to treat a wide range of health conditions, from cardiac problems to pain to cancer.

The University of Rochester Medical Center (URMC) has made the university the Greater Rochester area's largest employer since 2005, with more than 19,700 employees and a total budget of $1.7 billion. As a highly regarded research institution, URMC is responsible for numerous advances in the biomedical and health care fields.

The medical center's 739-bed Strong Memorial Hospital, one of Western New York's leading teaching hospitals, has a regional trauma center, highly regarded programs for the treatment of neuromuscular illnesses and cancer, women's health programs, and Western New York's only heart transplant program. Its emergency department treats more than 75,000 patients a year. Strong is also the site of Golisano Children's Hospital, one of the country's premier pediatric institutions, and has one of the few Ronald McDonald Houses located inside a hospital.

Highland Hospital, a URMC affiliate, first opened its doors on a hill near Highland Park in 1889 and is now known in part for a very modern service—bariatric surgery. Women's services include a maternity center and an inpatient unit devoted solely to women recovering from treatment related to breast cancer and gynecologic conditions. The 261-bed hospital, admitting more than 17,000 patients annually, also boasts a nationally ranked geriatrics program and orthopedic care center.

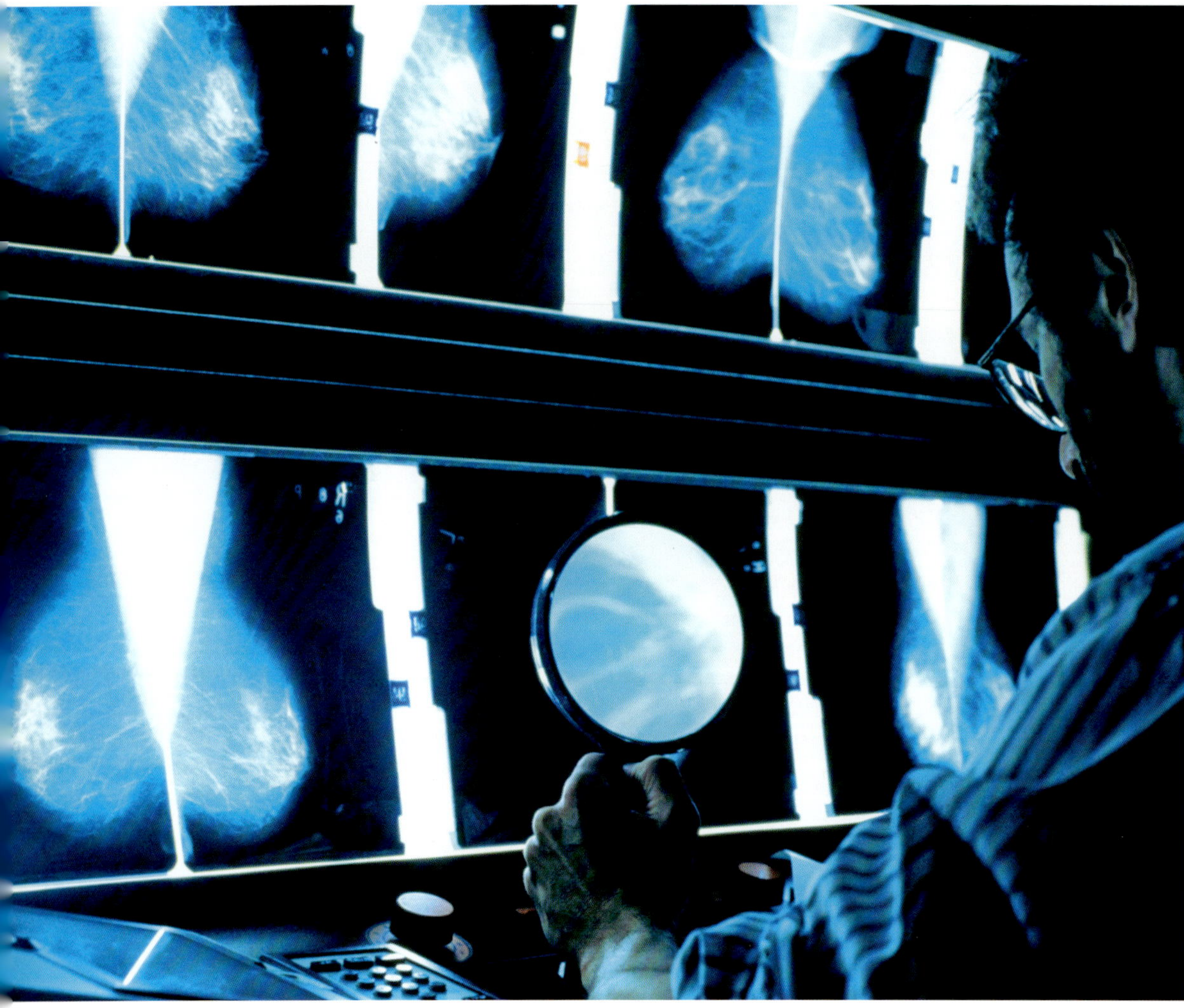

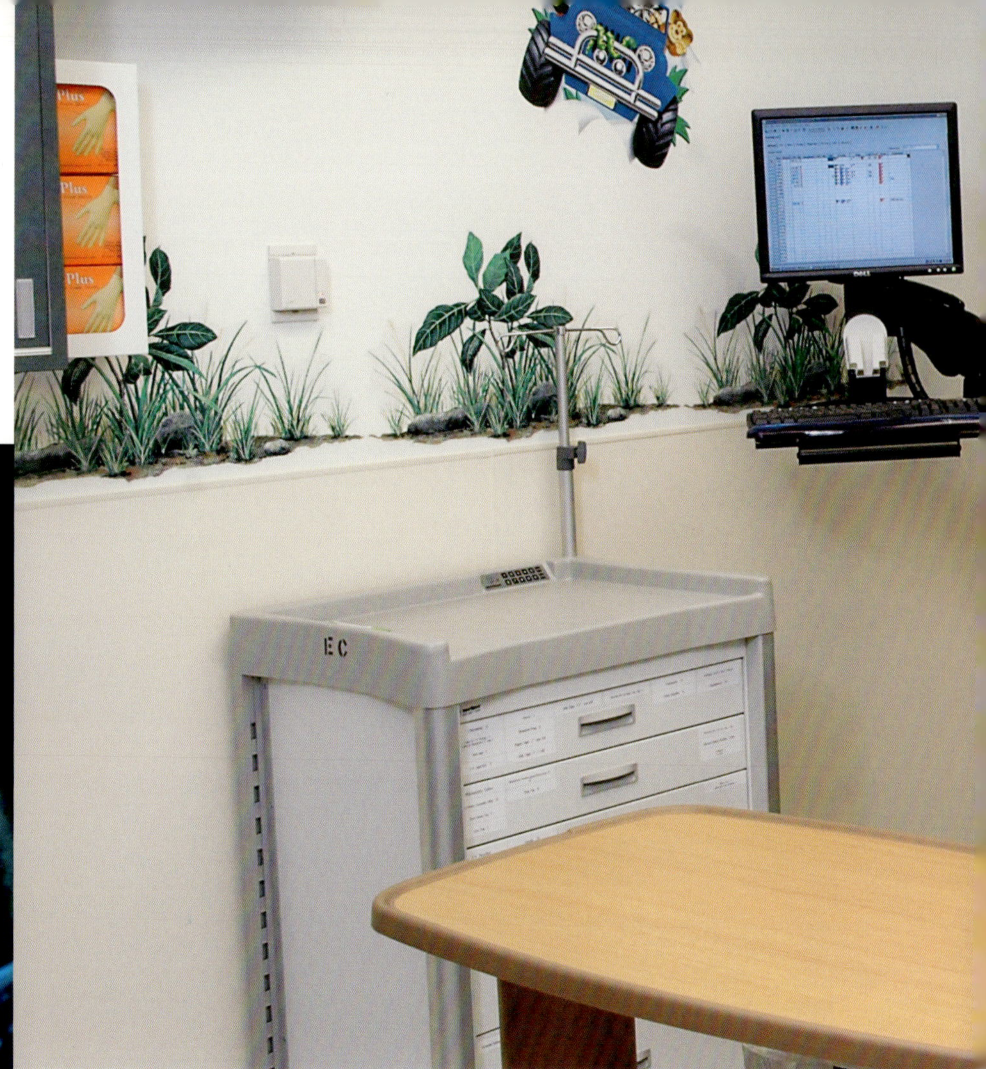

The Rochester Heart Institute at Rochester General Hospital is lauded as the region's only Solucient Top 100 Cardiovascular Hospital. Rochester General records some 1,700 cardiac surgeries and more than 6,800 diagnostic and intervention procedures each year and offers extensive patient counseling through its state-of-the-art rehabilitation program. The 528-bed hospital houses the Lipson Cancer Center, a regional leader specializing in cancer and blood disorders.

A major teaching hospital, Rochester General has a high-risk-pregnancy program, a special care nursery for newborns, an orthopedics program, pain-management

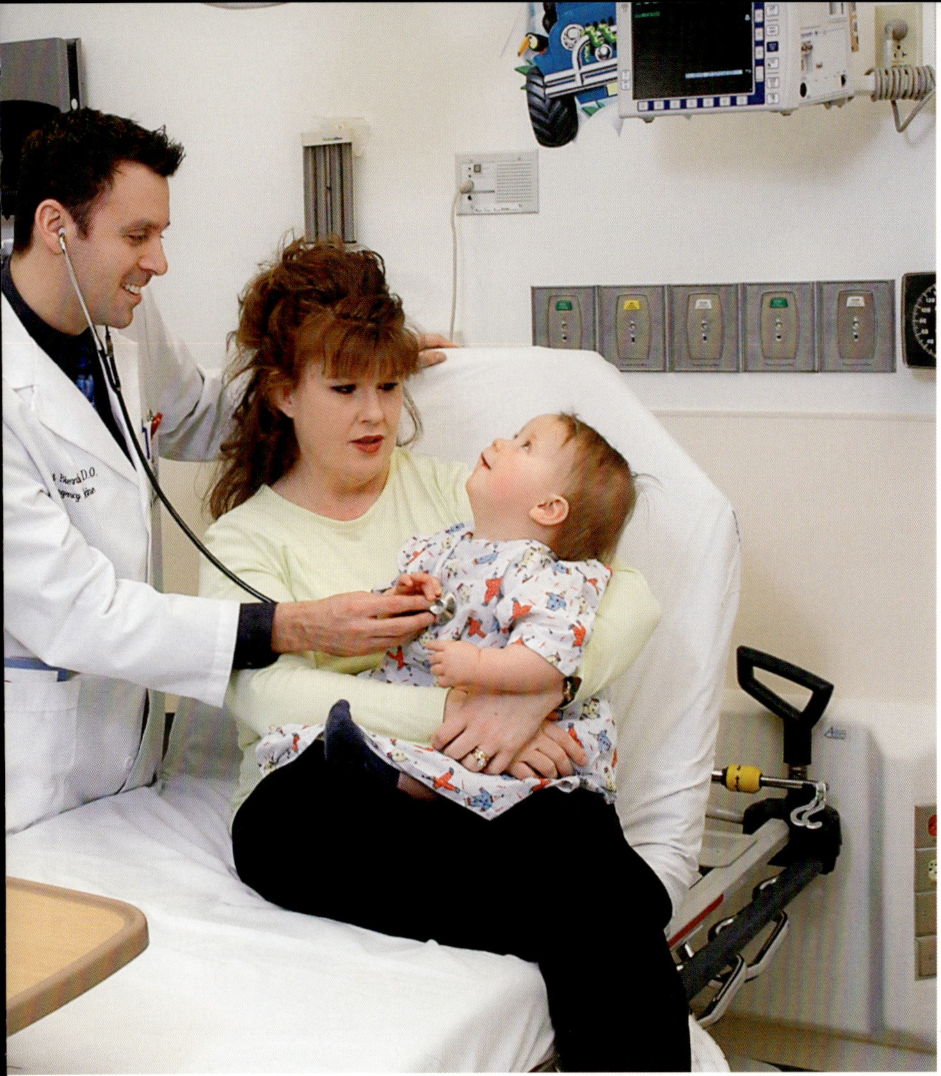

and behaviorial health services, and more. Its emergency department has more than 85,000 visits a year. Surgeons at Rochester General offer many types of minimally invasive surgery, and the hospital is a regional leader in robotic-assisted surgery. In July 2007, Rochester General and URMC announced a partnership to improve care for neurological patients, creating one of the country's largest joint stroke programs.

Specialized Centers

Rochester is home to one of the largest freestanding mammography and breast imaging centers in the nation, the Elizabeth Wende Breast Care clinic. Founded in 1975 by Dr. Wende Logan-Young, it is one of the top breast centers in the United States. The American College of Radiology has designated the clinic a Breast Imaging Center of Excellence. The clinic offers magnetic resonance imaging, mammography, and other diagnostic services and is involved in research.

Allergy Asthma Immunology of Rochester (AAIR) has been helping Rochester citizens breathe easier and feel better since 1985. The multispecialty group practice provides consultation and care for adults and children and is a teaching facility. Its infusion center provides treatment for arthritis, psoriasis, ulcerative colitis, Crohn's disease, and osteoporosis. With four locations, AAIR is one of the nation's largest practice-based sites for pharmaceutical-sponsored research.

For retirees, Jewish Senior *Life* offers accommodations for independent, enriched, or assisted living along with a variety of health care options at its 25-acre campus. The full continuum of care allows residents to advance from one level of care to another as needed without having to pay more for increased services.

Insuring Health

Among the area's top health insurers is Excellus BlueCross BlueShield, headquartered in Rochester and serving nearly two million members in 31 New York counties. Another large plan, Preferred Care, offers a network of some 4,500 physicians and other health professionals in the Greater Rochester area. It offers its members many programs to promote healthy living.

Rochester's wealth of academic and advanced health care offerings has created an educated, cultured, and vibrant community.

Opposite page, left: Studying a mammogram for signs of cancer; opposite page, right, and this page: A doctor of osteopathy examining a young patient at a Unity Health System facility.

This page: Downtown Rochester, with Bausch & Lomb headquarters in the center. Opposite page: Online banking with one of Rochester's many financial institutions.

CHAPTERFIVE

Professional and Business Services

ADVANCING THE ECONOMY AND THE COMMUNITY

Rochester has a robust support network of banks, professionals, contractors, and consultants committed to sustaining and advancing a vital community.

In addition to a full range of investment and banking services, the area's financial institutions pour millions of dollars into loans and grants that encourage affordable housing, economic development, neighborhood revitalization, and other public benefits.

The largest among them with ties to Western New York is Manufacturers and Traders Trust Company, known as M&T Bank and headquartered in Buffalo. Its parent company, M&T Bank Corporation, is one of the country's largest commercial bank holding companies, with more than 650 branches in the eastern United States, including more than 20 branches in the Rochester area.

Four other major financial institutions have established a commanding regional presence following the consolidation and buyouts of local, independent banks in the 1980s and 1990s. With 29 offices locally, JPMorgan Chase operates in more than 50 countries and has $1.5 trillion in assets. Operating approximately 22 branches in the Rochester area, HSBC–North America, with nearly $300 billion in assets, has some 400 branches in New York State. Bank of America, with 12 banking centers in Rochester itself and more in nearby communities, maintains branches in 175 countries and conducts business with 99 percent of U.S. Fortune 500 companies. Citizens Financial Group has assets of $159 billion and branches in 13 states, including five branches of its Citizens Bank in Rochester.

Several banks that got their start locally continue to grow. Demonstrating Canandaigua National Bank and Trust's long-standing reputation throughout the Rochester and Finger Lakes regions, the Ontario Children's Home has remained a customer since becoming the bank's first depositor in 1887, when it was known as the Ontario Orphan Asylum. The area's only full-service, locally owned community bank now offers services in 20 locations, has $1.2 billion in assets, and designs each branch to reflect the surrounding neighborhood.

ESL Federal Credit Union is the largest and strongest credit union in the state and among the top 1 percent of federally insured credit unions nationwide. Chartered by Eastman Kodak Company founder George Eastman as Eastman Savings and Loan Association in 1920, the progressive $3 billion institution has 19 branches in the Greater Rochester area and serves more than 285,000 members. It has broken ground on a new six-story, 180,000-square-foot headquarters building on Chestnut Street downtown, scheduled for completion in 2010.

Genesee Regional Bank, which got its start in 1996 and has two locations, serves small to medium-sized businesses and high-net-worth individuals. The bank recorded more than $100 million in assets in 2007.

The New Urban Landscape

After decades of talk and planning, multiple development projects are springing up and bringing people back downtown. Consultants hired by the city in 2007 projected steady development: between 156 and 309 new housing units yearly, with the potential for more, through 2015.

The Sagamore on East is one of the most striking additions to the heart of downtown's flourishing East End Cultural District. Offering seven stories of luxury condominiums atop retail and commercial space, the complex is a project of Christa Development Corporation, which has developed and built more than three million square feet of residential, commercial, and industrial space.

Opposite page, left: Rochester residents benefiting from the presence of some of the nation's largest financial institutions; opposite page, right: Canandaigua National Bank and Trust Company, one of the region's oldest banks. This page: The Sagamore on East, a recent condominium development in Rochester's East End Cultural District.

In historic Corn Hill, the Mark IV Construction Company in 2007 completed Corn Hill Landing—a mixture of upscale apartments, shops, and dining services that overlooks the city skyline and the Genesee River. Another riverside residential development, a revitalization project in planning for more than 20 years, is Brooks Landing—a $23 million combination of market-rate condominiums, a hotel, a restaurant, a coffeehouse, office space, and water access.

The Mills at High Falls, under construction downtown, will provide 67 affordable loft and town house–style units. Also planned are the Riverview Apartments, 120 units that will house University of Rochester students, and Conifer Realty's project to rehabilitate existing units and build 12 new residential buildings.

Rochester Renewal

A major change in the downtown commercial and business landscape is the planned 350,000-square-foot headquarters for PAETEC Holding Corp. It will be built on a portion of the site of the former Midtown Plaza, which closed in 2008. The PAETEC headquarters should be completed in 2012. A proposed project, Renaissance Square, with an anticipated $230 million price tag, would be the city center's main attraction and the biggest development project in Monroe County history. Plans for the seven-acre parcel include a bus terminal, a theater, retail space, and a satellite campus for Monroe Community College.

Grants from the U.S. Environmental Protection Agency to clean up brownfields will allow more development. One grant provides nearly $3.4 million to remediate environmental contamination at a former photographic film and paper manufacturing plant, which left behind large amounts of chemicals and waste.

This page, left: Staybridge Suites hotel under construction at Brooks Landing; this page, right, and opposite page, left: The Frederick Douglass–Susan B. Anthony Memorial Bridge seen from Corn Hill Landing. Opposite page, right: Buckingham Commons apartment and office building, redeveloped from a century-old former manufacturing facility.

Local residents collaborate with design professionals and planners through the Rochester Regional Community Design Center, which helps build walkable, sustainable neighborhoods as a partner in the growing New Urbanism movement. In 2006 the center began an annual series titled Reshaping Rochester! that uses lectures, exhibits, and leadership events to reshape and reinvigorate the city. In its inaugural season, the center won a community development award from the New York chapter of the American Institute of Architects.

Developers are also revamping many of downtown's old and vacant buildings to offer mixed-use opportunities to residents and business owners, restoring the

charm and character of some of the city's lost gems. Buckingham Properties took advantage of city and county incentives and financial assistance from Rochester Gas and Electric to transform a 103-year-old building into Buckingham Commons, seven stories of loft-style apartments and commercial space. The company also plans to invest more than $100 million to breathe new life into the 16.8-acre site of the former Genesee Hospital, a development now called Alexander Park. The company plans to demolish the vacant hospital building and construct a bank, offices, apartments, and retail space over several years.

Also specializing in the adaptive reuse of commercial properties is Costanza Enterprises, a family-owned management and investment company. Its more notable projects include the Temple Building, loft apartments in Rochester's only 20th-century neo-Gothic skyscraper, and Station 55, a blend of artist lofts and commercial space in a row of 19th-century brick warehouses.

Local architects, developers, and builders are tapped for projects elsewhere as well. The Pike Company has six locations in New York and Connecticut but maintains headquarters downtown in the same building where Dutch immigrant John Barnabas Pike opened shop in 1873. Four generations later, his descendants continue to put their architectural stamp on local treasures such as the Rochester Museum and Science Center and the archive rooms at the George Eastman House International Museum of Photography and Film. Among the company's major national projects are the Universe of Energy and World of Motion pavilions at Walt Disney World's Epcot Center.

A top design firm headquartered in Rochester is Clark Patterson Lee, with its team of architects, engineers, designers, and construction supervisors. The firm has offices throughout New York State and in Georgia, North Carolina,

and South Carolina. It handles a range of projects including commercial, industrial, environmental, transportation, educational, health care, and municipal facilities. Its many Rochester projects include a redesign at Rochester General Hospital and work on Interstates 490 and 590.

LeChase Construction, based in Rochester, has five regional offices in New York and North Carolina and specializes in civic, educational, and industrial facilities. LeChase completed roughly $450 million in building construction in 2007.

A Rochester staple for nearly 40 years, Billitier Electric has provided electrical contracting services for such clients as Wegmans Food Markets and the University of Rochester.

Opposite page, left: The Temple Building, a renovated 1925 neo-Gothic structure featuring commercial space and loft apartments; opposite page, right, and this page, left: Corporate offices of the Pike Company. This page, right: Hillside Children Center's Horton Family Center, a residential/medical center designed by Clark Patterson Lee.

Legal Expertise

Rochester has a broad range of legal firms with many areas of expertise. Some go back many decades, and some are national and international in scope.

Two of the country's most renowned law firms are based in Rochester. Harris Beach, ranked as one of the top 250 largest law firms in the United States, cut its legal teeth in a small downtown office in 1856. The firm has since grown to nearly 200 attorneys across New York. Nixon Peabody is one of the country's largest multipractice law firms, with roughly 700 attorneys in 16 cities and a Rochester location dating back to 1875.

Harter Secrest & Emery's lineage can be traced to 1893, when the firm's founders formed a professional relationship with Eastman Kodak. Bausch & Lomb was also another early client. These and many other long-term relationships continue to this day. The firm's headquarters are in Rochester.

The law firm of Boylan, Brown, Code, Vigdor & Wilson provides guidance to start-ups and emerging technology companies. The attorneys help structure financing plans, establish intellectual property rights, and protect other key assets for clients.

This page, left: Rochester attorneys practicing law in some of the nation's oldest and largest firms; this page, right: Taking the pulse of a city in an opinion poll on

Helping Businesses Thrive

Rochester expertise and innovation provide services that help businesses thrive. Harris Interactive, one of the largest market research firms in the world, is headquartered in Rochester, with offices around the globe. Known for the Harris Poll, the company provides online research and other services that help companies understand what drives their customers' decisions. The company was formed in 1996 when the Gordon S. Black Corporation, established in Rochester in 1975, purchased Louis Harris and Associates, founded by Lou Harris, who was President John F. Kennedy's pollster.

For full-service marketing communications, Dixon Schwabl has been serving Rochester businesses and institutions since 1987. The firm has more than 90 clients. In 2008 the Great Place to Work Institute named Dixon Schwabl the best small company to work for in America. The company donates thousands of hours each year in promotion and fund-raising for not-for profits.

Payroll service is another area where Rochester innovation has paid off. Before B. Thomas Golisano became a billionaire philanthropist and three-time gubernatorial candidate, he approached the payroll processing company he worked for with a plan to make its services easier and more affordable for small businesses. When his employer was not interested, he decided to execute the plan himself. In 1971, with just one employee and $3,000, Golisano launched Paychex. Headquartered in Rochester, Paychex now serves more than 572,000 businesses, has more than 100 locations across the country, and recorded revenues exceeding $1.9 billion in fiscal 2007.

BlueTie is one of the fastest-growing software providers in the world, offering e-mail, calendar, and other organization and collaboration services to small and midsized businesses. The privately held company, founded in 1999 by David Koretz and Paychex's Golisano, distributes those services on the retail end through direct and Internet sales, and on the wholesale end through 650 resellers and Internet service providers.

For professional, financial, and support services, Rochester leads the way with innovation, stellar quality, and a broad range of providers and applications. It is another means by which Rochester provides the competitive edge that keeps businesses growing.

This page: At General Motors' Honeoye Falls facility, preparing for the start of the first 300-mile, non-emission-producing and nonrefueling journey of a fuel-cell vehicle, May 15, 2007. Opposite page: Inspecting a canola crop, a source of biodiesel fuel.

Energy, Transportation, and Communications

MOVING FORWARD

Affordable, reliable energy, efficient transportation, and high-tech communications are key factors in a community's economic success. Rochester has them all.

New Energy

At a time when energy is a top economic issue, local organizations and businesses are developing alternative-energy technologies as a thriving new industry. Fuel cells in particular hold tremendous promise for the Rochester region, which has become a national leader in alternative-energy research and development. Dozens of companies have been drawn to the area for its rich agricultural resources and an expert science-driven workforce doing groundbreaking work in this emerging industry, one that is expected to be worth as much as $160 million by 2016. Rochester has the expertise to support these endeavors. Area colleges and universities grant more than 1,200 engineering and related diplomas each year, and nearly 60 percent of the region's 85,000 manufacturing workers are in high-tech jobs.

Local economic development organizations offer a significant number of incentive programs available to businesses specializing in fuel cells and alternative energy. As a result, the area's technological expertise in the development of fuel cells—including thin films, ceramics, and microelectronic systems—has lifted Rochester to the top in a market bulging with opportunities to bring those cells from the laboratory to the masses.

Generations-old contributions in automotive history have laid the groundwork for pioneering work at General Motors (GM) and Delphi, two of the world's largest auto suppliers, which run their largest fuel-cell research facilities in the region.

GM, which has spent more than $1 billion in fuel-cell research and development, operates a Fuel Cell Development Center—one of only four such GM centers around the globe—in the nearby village of Honeoye Falls. Local researchers, who focus on proton exchange membrane fuel cells, worked on GM's Hy-Wire concept car, a fuel-cell vehicle unveiled in 2002. Rochester is participating in the company's Project Driveway program, the first comprehensive market test of fuel-cell vehicles.

Researchers at Delphi Technical Center Rochester in West Henrietta focus on solid oxide and proton exchange membrane fuel cells. In 2001 the U.S. Department of Energy awarded Delphi a 10-year, $138 million solid oxide fuel-cell project, much of which is being carried out at Delphi's 330,000-square-foot facility.

Numerous other local companies are advancing the fuel-cell technology market as well. Among them is Eastman Kodak Company, which is helping New York–based Medis Technologies produce fuel cells for portable consumer products, while Harris RF Communications Division is developing direct-methanol fuel cells for military tactical radios.

Area schools of higher education invest heavily in fuel-cell research and development. The University of Rochester (U of R) has budgeted more than $50 million for research and development to rank among the leading universities in this field. In April 2007, the university announced the creation of the Nanosystems Initiative, a federally funded, $1.8 million nanotechnology research center dedicated to developing fuel cells and optical biosensors.

In 2004 the Rochester Institute of Technology (RIT) became a Hydrogen Technology Learning Center, one of only four such centers nationwide funded by the U.S. Department of Energy. RIT's Advanced Fuel Cell Research Laboratory received $1.35 million in federal funding in 2006 to study fuel-cell lifecycles, their environmental impact, and their disposal—information necessary for developing fuel cells for mainstream consumer and commercial products. RIT also serves as home base for Renewable Energy Network of Entrepreneurs in Western New York, a program that offers alternative energy

start-ups assistance with education and training, grants and awards, networking, and other services.

From Farmland to Fuel

Rochester's farms grow many of the crops that are used for fuel. With such ample supplies, the region has become home to biofuel ethanol and biodiesel research and production facilities that are leading the way in biological fuels. One of those plants is the only producer of the vegetable oil–based fuel in Upstate New York. Located in Ontario, Wayne County, and owned by Northern Biodiesel, it has the capacity to produce 7.5 million gallons of biodiesel a year.

Western New York Energy has invested $87 million to develop New York's first state-of-the-art dry mill ethanol plant in Shelby, Orleans County, where up to 50 million gallons of clean-burning, fuel-grade ethanol will be produced each year. Operational since early 2008, the 144-acre plant also is expected to turn out 95,000 tons of carbon dioxide and 250,000 tons of distillers' grains annually. The company, which received nearly $6 million in state funding to build the facility, will buy approximately six million bushels of corn each year to make the ethanol.

Contributing to the alternative-fuel effort is Genencor International, one of the country's leading biotechnology companies. The Rochester-based firm is a worldwide producer of enzymes and other bioproducts that help make ethanol and lessen the environmental impact of the cleaning, textile, fuel, and chemical industries.

Opposite page, left: Discussion at the Rochester Institute of Technology on the advantages of using green technology in vehicle production. Opposite page, right,

The New York State Agricultural Experiment Station in Geneva, Ontario County, is a world leader in agricultural research and development. Affiliated with Cornell University, the station supports biofuels technology, including the production of next-generation cellulosic ethanol (made from cellulose).

Also in Geneva, the Cornell Agriculture and Food Technology Park is a unique site that allows food, agriculture, and bio-based companies to collaborate with Cornell University researchers. The 72-acre research park has facilities for research, development, and light production, and the collaboration helps move bio-based innovations from the laboratory to the private sector for eventual commercial use.

This page, left: Cornell Agriculture and Food Technology Park in Geneva; this page, right: Wind turbines providing an alternative source of energy to Western New York. Opposite page, left: Hands-on training at Gleason Corporation; opposite page, right: High Falls on the Genesee River, a source of hydroelectric power in

Sustainable Energy

Wind turbines are generating interest as well as electricity in Rochester. As part of its sustainability initiative, local manufacturer Diamond Packaging has made a commitment to purchase 100 percent wind energy. In nearby Wyoming County, the 10-turbine, 6.6-megawatt Wethersfield Wind Farm, which covers 310 acres, has been operational since 2000. Several other wind farms are in the works.

One of Rochester's oldest manufacturers, Gleason Corporation makes equipment that Hansen Transmissions uses to build gears for wind turbines. Hansen, headquartered in Europe, is a global leader in its field. Many other companies in the Rochester region have the specialized capabilities for manufacturing various components for wind turbines, which contribute to a multibillion-dollar wind and solar energy industry growing by double digits every year.

Traditional energy supplier Rochester Gas and Electric (RG&E) offers its 360,000 electricity customers the opportunity to purchase wind-generated electricity. From 2006 to 2007, the company reports, participating customers used nearly 34 million kilowatt hours of wind-generated electricity. The utility, which serves nine counties, also provides funding to promote economic development in the region to attract and retain business. It also offers programs that reward businesses for cutting electrical use during high-demand periods.

In the solar energy field, a top innovator is Wakonda Technologies in Perinton, which develops proprietary technology for military and commercial use. In 2007 the company outdid hundreds of applicants to be named the Clean Energy Entrepreneur of the Year at an industry forum sponsored by the U.S. Department of Energy's National Renewable Energy Laboratory. The award recognized the commercialization of an aesthetically pleasing, lighter-weight system for converting sunlight into electricity.

An even broader environmental initiative comes from the city itself. Backed by the U.S. Green Building Council, Rochester is working to become the nation's first green city, based on leadership in community-supported, environmentally friendly technologies, buildings, and infrastructure. Already designated as the site of the country's first Hydrogen Village, Rochester plans hydrogen production, distribution, and refueling centers that will harness energy from the city's downtown waterfall to power fuel-cell cars, buses, and some downtown buildings. In the suburb of East Rochester, the school district's use of fuel cells is expected to save the district as much as $100,000 annually in energy costs.

Getting Here and There

An international airport, railways, a statewide highway, and three interstates help make Rochester an easy place to do business. The Greater Rochester International Airport (GRIA) connects Western New York to cities in the Northeast and to major hubs in the Midwest, with nine major airlines handling 220 flights daily to more than 20 cities and serving roughly 2.5 million passengers annually. Five air cargo shippers include DHL Worldwide and Federal Express. Recently renovated, the airport generates nearly $500 million a year for the local economy.

Amtrak's Rochester location records more than 76,000 boardings and alightings annually. The city is on the train's Empire Service route, which also covers New York City, Albany, Syracuse, Buffalo, and Niagara Falls. Rail freight services are provided by Rochester & Southern Railroad, Norfolk Southern, Canadian Pacific, and CSX, which has rail-to-truck transloading for bulk products.

The area trucking industry provides intermodal transport and freight brokerage. Marine freight services are offered at the Port of Rochester, from which vessels make their way to the St. Lawrence Seaway before reaching the Atlantic Ocean.

Rochester offers excellent highway access. The New York State Thruway has three exits serving Rochester, and at 496 miles is the longest toll road in the country. Interstate 390 is a north-south auxiliary highway that spans nearly 75 miles and connects to the Thruway in the southern suburb of Henrietta. Just outside downtown Rochester, the northern tip of I-390 meets up with Interstate 490, a major east-west highway running through the middle of the city and connecting to the Thruway on each end. At a mere five miles long, Interstate 590 runs along the southeast border of the city, connects I-490 to the north and I-390 to the south, and is a spur of the Thruway.

Opposite page: Boarding for a cross-country flight at the Greater Rochester International Airport. This page, left: A Genesee & Wyoming freight train, part of the Rochester & Southern Railroad, loading up at the American Rock Salt mine at Hampton Corners, New York; this page, right: On the Keeler Expressway, Route 104, which runs east and west through the northern part of the city.

High-Tech Connections

Rochester is well connected, with telephone and Internet service providers offering a variety of services. A major telecommunications services provider headquartered in Rochester is One Communications, which provides telephone, Internet, and related services to more than 160,000 businesses in 16 states and the District of Columbia. Services also include T1 lines, private networks, Web hosting, wireless options, telephone, and more.

Frontier Communications, which goes back nearly a century, today offers state-of-the-art telecommunications products and services, including local and long-distance access, high-speed Internet access, and satellite television. Frontier recently launched a number of free wireless zones in the Rochester area. The company has three million subscribers in 24 states.

Poised to make its mark on the Rochester skyline is one of the fastest-growing technology companies in the United States. PAETEC Holding Corp., which provides communications services to medium- and large-sized businesses, plans to build its 350,000-square-foot headquarters downtown, moving existing personnel from nearby Perinton and eventually adding more jobs.

Other telecommunications companies with a significant regional presence include Verizon, Time Warner, and Global Crossing, an international company with 500 workers in Rochester, its largest location.

For energy, transportation, and communications, Rochester is on the cutting edge with technology and service. It has the systems a business needs to grow and prosper.

PART TWO

CHAMPIONS OF COMMERCE: PROFILES OF COMPANIES AND ORGANIZATIONS

PROFILES OF COMPANIES AND ORGANIZATIONS

Agribusiness and Food Processing

Constellation Brands, Inc.

Headquartered in upstate New York for more than 60 years, this leading international producer and marketer of beverage alcohol brands has a broad portfolio of wine, imported beer, and spirits. It markets more than 250 brands in nearly 150 countries in North America, South America, Europe, and the Asia-Pacific region.

Above: Constellation Brands, Inc. offers more than 250 brands in its wine, imported beer, and spirits portfolio and has sales in approximately 150 countries.

What began in 1945 as Canandaigua Industries Company—a firm selling barrels of bulk wine to bottlers in the eastern United States—has grown to become the largest wine producer in the world. Today named Constellation Brands, Inc., with headquarters in Fairport, New York, the company is a leading international producer and marketer of beverage alcohol in the wine, imported beer, and spirits categories.

Major names in the Constellation Brands portfolio include Robert Mondavi, Clos du Bois, Ravenswood, Blackstone, Hardys, Kim Crawford, Inniskillin, and Ruffino wines; Corona Extra, Modelo Especial, Negro Modelo, and Pacifico beers; and Effen Vodka, Black Velvet Canadian Whisky, and SVEDKA Vodka.

Founded in Canandaigua, New York, the company has grown organically and through acquisitions across all segments of the beverage alcohol industry, while maintaining its roots and a significant presence in upstate New York. Constellation Brands employs approximately 9,200 people globally, including about 600 in the Rochester area.

A Rich History in Upstate New York

More than 60 years ago, 21-year-old Marvin Sands founded the Canandaigua Industries Company in a former sauerkraut factory located in the Finger Lakes region of New York. In that first year, the company employed eight people and sold 200,000 gallons of wine that grossed $150,000 in sales.

During the next few decades, with founder Sands at the helm, the company grew significantly, it became publicly traded, and its name evolved to become the Canandaigua Wine Company. In the 1970s and 1980s the founder's sons, Richard and Rob, took prominent roles with the company. In 1993, with the purchase of Barton Incorporated, the company became the first major wine producer in the United States to diversify into the imported beer and distilled spirits categories.

Then, in 1998 the company spanned the Atlantic with its first European acquisition, the purchase of Matthew Clark, plc, one of the United Kingdom's leading producers and marketers of wine, cider, and bottled water. The purchase expanded Canandaigua Wine's portfolio to include brands such as Stone's Ginger Wine, which dates back to the 18th century. Matthew Clark was—and remains—the United Kingdom's largest independent drinks wholesaler. This part of its business became part of a joint venture with Punch Taverns in 2007.

In 2000 the Canandaigua Wine Company was renamed Constellation Brands, Inc. to reflect the scope of the company, its broad range of products across the beverage alcohol market segments, and its aspiration to have a stellar stable of top brands. Since that time, Constellation Brands has continued to grow by adding a number of premium assets to its global portfolio, including Ravenswood, Blackstone, Australia's BRL Hardy, the storied wines from Robert Mondavi, Canada's Vincor International, and the Clos du Bois and Wild Horse brands and wineries, among others. The company also acquired Effen Vodka and SVEDKA Vodka. In addition, it entered into a joint venture with Grupo Modelo to form Crown Imports, which imports and markets brands such as Corona beer throughout the entire United States.

In 2006 Constellation Brands produced 110 million cases of wine and recorded $5.2 billion in net sales for the fiscal year ending February 28, 2007. Constellation Brands (NYSE: STZ), a Fortune 500 company, is included in the Standard & Poor's 500 Index. Constellation Brands continues to set its sights on opportunities for organic and acquisition growth. The company provides additional information about its products and activities on its Web site (www.cbrands.com).

"In the five years from 2002 to 2007, Constellation Brands's net sales doubled, and through our established 'True Growth' strategy, we are focused on harvesting long-term profitable growth opportunities with returns that exceed our cost of capital," states Rob Sands, president and CEO. "Consumers are trading up to premium wines, beers, and spirits, and our strategy is to seek opportunities that meet their preferences and our targets for creating shareholder value."

Investing in the Community

Since its founding, Constellation Brands has maintained a deep sense of pride in giving back to the community. This sense of pride, as well as responsibility, is true to the company's core values established by Marvin Sands. In the Rochester metropolitan area, Constellation Brands is a supporter of EnCompass: Resources for Learning, ViaHealth, and Rochester General Hospital, the Norman Howard School, the Harley School, Rochester Philharmonic Orchestra, American Red Cross, Memorial Art Gallery of the University of Rochester, United Way, Seneca Park Zoo, Thompson Health System and Strong Health System, and other worthy organizations. It also is a founding member of the New York Wine & Culinary Center, which was opened in 2006, and the Constellation Brands–Marvin Sands Performing Arts Center (CMAC) at Finger Lakes Community College in Canandaigua.

"When my father started the company more than 60 years ago, he was a staunch supporter in not only preserving the land from which our products originate but also giving back to our communities," Rob Sands says. "His vision and values continue to guide the company today in our decision making and planning for the future."

Constellation Brands Rankings

Constellation Brands is a leader in numerous marketing categories.

- Largest wine producer by volume in the world
- Largest wine company in the United States based on sales dollar value
- Largest wine company in the United Kingdom, Australia, and Canada
- Second-largest wine company in New Zealand
- Largest beer importer and marketer in the United States through its Crown Imports joint venture with Mexico's Grupo Modelo
- Third-largest U.S. beverage alcohol company based on retail sales in the food and drug channels

Above left: The corporate headquarters of Constellation Brands—a leading international producer and marketer of wine—is located in the Finger Lakes region of New York State. Above right: For more than 60 years, Marvin Sands, center, and subsequently his sons Rob, left, and Richard have led the company. By 2003, Constellation Brands had become the largest wine producer in the world.

PROFILES OF COMPANIES AND ORGANIZATIONS

Construction, Development, Architecture, and Engineering

Clark Patterson Lee

This innovative firm of design professionals provides clients with comprehensive design and construction services of exceptional quality and value while promoting both corporate and individual growth. The firm's multidiscipline staff manages every aspect of each project with personal attention and principal participation.

Above left: For Rochester General Hospital, one of Clark Patterson Lee's many notable projects, the firm focused primarily on the realignment of patient care and special care programs, providing an innovative building transformation. Above right: The Parkview Drive Bridge design project combined the shoring up of the bridge while maintaining its aesthetic appeal. Top right: Redesign and renovation expanded the University of North Carolina–Asheville Highsmith University Center to more than twice its original size.

Chances are most people have come across a Clark Patterson Lee project somewhere in the Rochester area and in the northeastern and southeastern United States. When a faucet is turned on, the water could be flowing through a municipal system developed by Clark Patterson Lee engineers and planners.

A bridge, a parking garage, a hospital, a local middle school, a neighborhood church, or a favorite museum—any of these structures could be the result of the efforts of the Clark Patterson Lee team. In fact, the professionals at Clark Patterson Lee represent such a wide range of expertise, they could literally create a city—from the earliest planning stages to final construction—applying the same care, consideration, and thoughtful approach clients are accustomed to receiving from the firm on strategic, everyday projects.

With more than 12 offices in the Northeast and the Southeast, Clark Patterson Lee is a leading provider of a full array of high quality planning, architecture, engineering, and construction management services.

History and Roots in Rochester

Founded more than 30 years ago, the firm has maintained a commitment to design quality, believing in the value of full-service capability while developing a comprehensive approach to meet each client's specific needs. A diverse team of more than 200 skilled individuals works to improve a client's built environment and strengthen their business, while remaining responsible stewards of the natural environment.

Clark Patterson Lee enjoys a rich history in the Rochester region, from the firm's earliest days as Clark Engineers, serving the Hudson Valley and upstate New York in the mid 1970s, to the present day, with offices in Georgia and in North and South Carolina. Projects include award-winning initiatives in education, health care, industry and commerce, public works, transportation, and community planning. Museums, municipal buildings, and efforts in the faith community are among the specialty projects taken on by Clark Patterson Lee.

The Firm Today

Clark Patterson Lee employees work to meet today's challenges to create stronger communities for tomorrow. Clark Patterson Lee is behind many beloved projects in Rochester and across the Northeast and Southeast. Projects in Rochester include additions and master plans at several major hospitals as well as construction of schools.

In the education sector, Clark Patterson Lee has worked on elementary schools, colleges and universities, charter schools, and day care centers. It has designed courthouses and art museums, including creating the master plan for the Mint Museum of Art in Charlotte, North Carolina. It has also worked on facilities at the University of North Carolina at Chapel Hill and Charlotte Country Day School.

The Team

The team at Clark Patterson Lee represents a diverse group of employees, with backgrounds in a variety of fields. In Rochester and 11 other locations, Clark Patterson Lee's talented team members represent nearly every discipline in architecture, planning, engineering, and construction services. These conscientious and experienced professionals provide a hands-on approach to every project. This personal approach is a hallmark of Clark Patterson Lee and dates back to the firm's origins in Rochester and continues to this day in the ranks of the more than 200 team members working with clients across the network of offices.

"The team at Clark Patterson Lee is talented and diverse, with a strong commitment to the communities we live and work in," states Phillip J. Clark, founder and chairman of Clark Patterson Lee. "As our firm has evolved over three decades, we have built a multidisciplined staff, reflecting the regions we serve. It is wonderful to experience the growth and development of the Northeast and the Southeast, all under the watch of our team here at Clark Patterson Lee."

Giving Back

The Clark Patterson Lee approach encourages employees to give back to the community, with employees volunteering their time and talent to a number of philanthropic organizations. In Rochester this includes collecting holiday gifts for Hillside Children's Center, supporting many charitable events throughout the year, and giving employees the opportunity to take time off to volunteer for a charitable organization of their choice.

In all of its sectors, Clark Patterson Lee is known for its generosity and community spirit. "We are proud of our firm's efforts to help others in the community. It is rewarding to see staff members embrace charitable causes with the same enthusiasm they bring to clients' projects," states Todd M. Liebert, AIA, NCARB, president of Clark Patterson Lee. The firm supports many professional organizations on behalf of its employees, including leadership positions in American Institute of Architects (AIA) chapters across the Northeast and the Southeast, while mentoring interns and young leaders in each of its offices.

Clark Patterson Lee's myriad of projects includes education, health care, environmental, municipal, specialty, industrial, commercial, transportation, and community planning. Top left: The Gananda Central School District's new Ruben A. Cirillo High School takes advantage of modern architectural concepts. Top center: PeopleSoft Animal Care and Education Center Humane Society at Lollypop Farm benefits from Clark Patterson Lee's wide-ranging expertise. Top right: The Hillside Children's Center's new Horton Family Center is a residential/medical center. Bottom left: Shown here during reconstruction is Interstate 490 Eastern Expressway and the Interstate 590 Outer Loop interchange in Rochester. Bottom right: The JCC's Wolk Children's Center is a state-of-the-art facility.

Billitier Electric, Inc.

Expert at performing a wide range of electrical services, Billitier Electric, Inc. is committed to satisfying each client's requirements and timelines. This dedication and consistent level of high performance has enabled the company to become one of the largest single-source electrical contractors in Western New York.

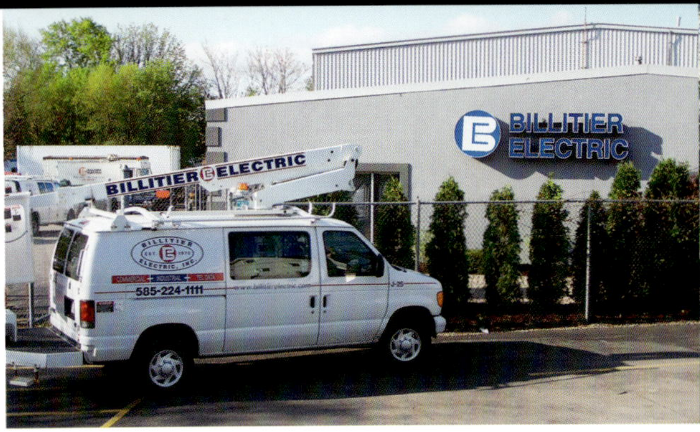

Above left: Billitier Electric, Inc. headquarters is located in Rochester, New York. Above right: Shown is a sample of Billitier's fleet of service vehicles.

Billitier Electric, Inc. is driven by its dedication to excellence and to continually improving its products and services. Its record of providing quality work has enabled it to grow from a midsize operation begun by Ron and Helen Billitier in their Rochester home in 1970 to one of Western New York's most significant single-source commercial and industrial electrical contractors. In 1995 the Billitiers' son Ron Jr. assumed the helm of the company as president and owner, ensuring that the company will continue to grow and succeed well into the future.

Throughout the year, Billitier employs an average of 125 electricians; it is a signatory contractor with the International Brotherhood of Electrical Workers (IBEW). The company's fully qualified teams build complete electrical systems for medical centers, schools, grocery and retail stores, sports stadiums, factories, and warehouses.

Billitier installs underground cabling, computer networks, security systems, and fire alarms. The company also installs an array of sophisticated fiber-optic and telecommunications components. Its teams can lay out networks consisting of a single cable to unlimited numbers of cables, in small offices or large commercial buildings. Billitier's teams are also proficient at performing cost-saving retrofitting, including replacing equipment and upgrading systems, as well as factory line maintenance.

Billitier estimators use the latest, most sophisticated systems designed to sharpen estimates and eliminate surprises. The maintenance department deploys top-of-the-line boom-bucket and sky-bucket trucks, infrared scanners for checking older facilities and preventing unexpected shutdowns, and all other equipment that is necessary to perform the required work. The communications department is just a phone call away 24 hours a day, as is an emergency repair vehicle rigged with a fusion splicer, optical time-domain reflectometer (OTDR), and equipment for repairing fiber optics.

To ensure that systems will operate smoothly in the long term, Billitier design teams use state-of-the-art software to create complete electrical systems, from heating, ventilation, and air-conditioning (HVAC) controls to local area network (LAN) wiring, and they work closely with clients from initial concept to finished drawings. Updates are performed quickly and efficiently, and the customer is provided with full documentation.

Billitier has established itself as the primary electrical contractor for the store maintenance and construction of a leading northeast supermarket chain. Billitier performs complete design-build work on many of Wegmans' new projects, retrofits, and upgrades. As Wegmans has grown and expanded its operations out of Western New York, Billitier has grown along with this leading supermarket chain.

Billitier also has a longtime association with the University of Rochester. In March 2007 the company completed work on Goergen Hall—a new biomedical engineering and optics building on the university's River Campus, with lecture halls, classrooms, and computer and seminar rooms, and 26,000 square feet of dedicated laboratory space. Other projects at the University of Rochester include electrical installations for the 163,000-square-foot James P. Wilmot Cancer Center and performing electrical work at Highland Hospital.

Billitier's office is located in Rochester, New York. The company covers project sites in upstate and Western New York, northern Pennsylvania, and New Jersey. More information about the company is available on its Web site at www.billitierelectric.com.

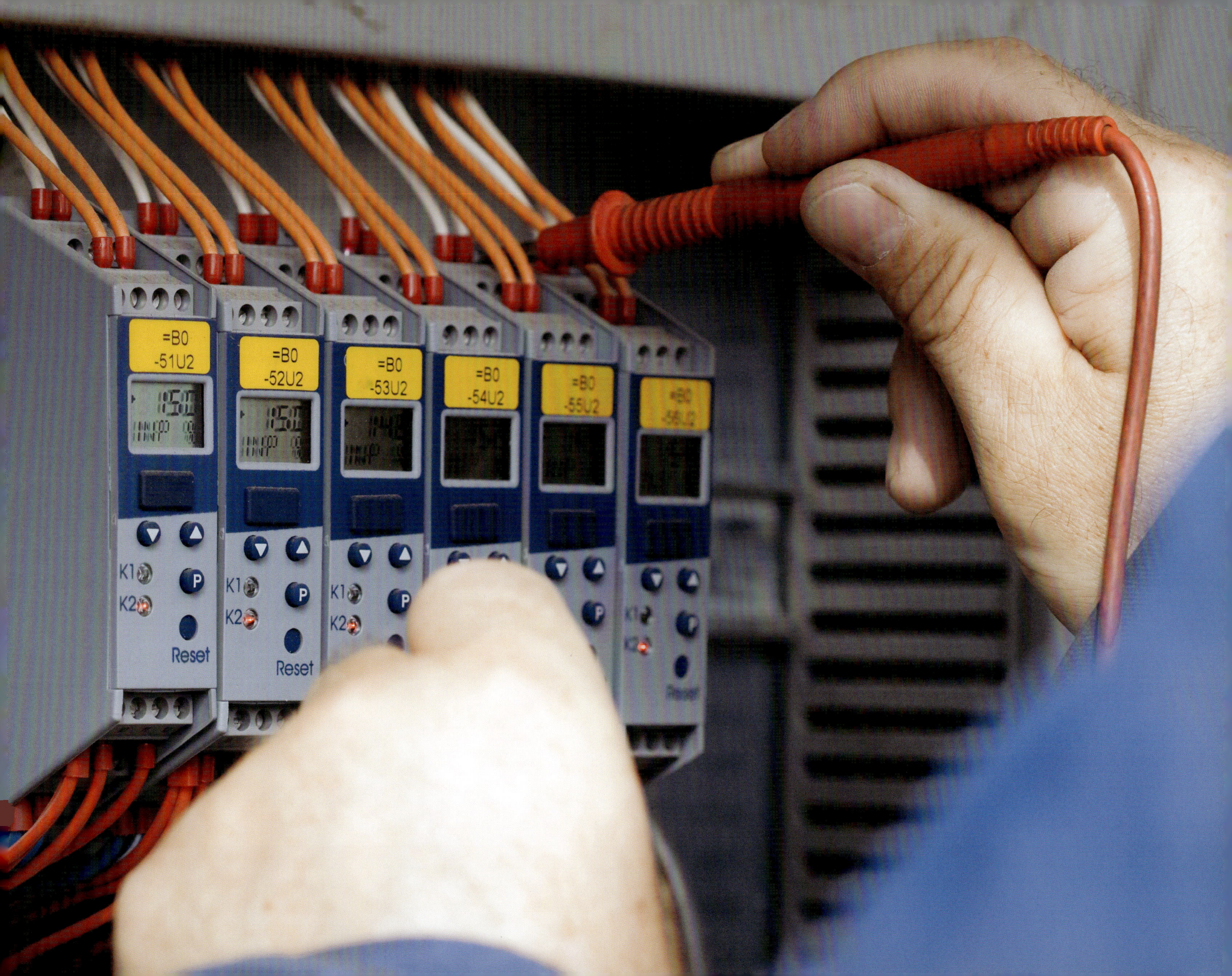
=B0
-51U2
=B0
-52U2
=B0
-53U2
=B0
-54U2
=B0
-55U2
K1
K2
P
Reset
K1
K2
P
Reset

PROFILES OF COMPANIES AND ORGANIZATIONS

Education

The College at Brockport, State University of New York

This educational institution is a selective, state-supported, four-year comprehensive college with programs blending the liberal arts with professional studies. The college's 464-acre wooded campus is located in Brockport, New York, on the historic Erie Canal.

Above: Picturesque Hartwell Garden provides a quiet and lovely place where students at The College at Brockport, State University of New York (SUNY) can stroll or study. Above right: Brockport's $18 million student town homes support student learning with comfortable apartment-style living, complete with wireless Internet access.

The College at Brockport, State University of New York (SUNY), located on the western edge of the Greater Rochester area in the Victorian village of Brockport, is rich in history and tradition. A founding member of the SUNY system, the college can trace its roots back to 1835, when the original Brockport Collegiate Institute first opened its doors. Honoring its legacy as a leader in innovative academic programs and a champion of student success, Brockport is committed to offering a multidimensional education that leads to a life of fulfillment and accomplishment by making students active partners in their intellectual, physical, and creative development.

Today Brockport serves nearly 7,000 undergraduate and 1,400 graduate students and offers 47 undergraduate programs, 29 graduate programs, and 23 areas of teacher certification. A recognized leader in academic excellence, Brockport offers many programs that have received national accreditation. The quality of the student body at Brockport is also exceptional. The class of 2011 has an average SAT score of 1117 and an average ACT score of 24, and its students were among the top 9 percent of their high school graduating class. Although selective, the college also offers several avenues to higher education, including the Educational Opportunity Program and the Rochester Educational Opportunity Center in downtown Rochester, which provide both career and college preparatory programs. Many transfer students—more than 900 in 2007—from community colleges and other four-year institutions find Brockport to be an outstanding choice to continue their education.

Graduate studies at Brockport offer an array of quality master's degrees and advanced study programs to meet the needs of the Rochester region's professional workforce. Programs in business, social work, public administration, education, environmental science, computer science, history, English, dance, photography, and more make the college the area's largest public graduate school. With an eye toward workforce demand and national and regional trends, Brockport offers innovative programs that serve the Rochester community.

National publications have also taken notice of Brockport. *Kiplinger's Personal Finance* included the college in its top "100 Best Values in Public Colleges" in the United States based on top-flight academics and affordability. The college is ranked in the top 100 in The Princeton Review's "America's Best Value Colleges" and "Best Colleges in the Northeast," and it also was ranked among the top master's universities in the North in *U.S.News & World Report*'s "America's Best Colleges" guide.

An enduring strength of Brockport is its faculty members who, through their focus on teaching, research, and service, act as extraordinary role models for their students. With 94 percent of faculty holding the highest degrees in their fields, Brockport faculty and emeriti include 15 Fulbright scholars, 26 SUNY Distinguished Faculty, 90 recipients of the Chancellor's Award for Excellence in Teaching, and six recipients of the Chancellor's Award for Scholarship and Creativity. The student-to-faculty ratio at Brockport is 18 to one, and the average class size is 22, ensuring that students receive individual attention. Faculty also serve as academic advisors and mentors, helping students to tailor their educational experiences and shape their academic and professional goals. This collegial community promotes responsibility, tolerance, and respect, providing students with critical service-learning opportunities as they, too, serve on various committees and boards, becoming productive team players and effective leaders.

Brockport's distinctive programs provide students with a balanced and rigorous liberal arts education, including one of the most expansive study abroad programs in the country. With 65 opportunities in more than 20 countries, students gain first-hand experience of a diverse and increasingly interconnected world. The Honors Program and the Delta College Program provide unique learning experiences for those students seeking additional academic challenges and opportunities for personal development. The Honors Program offers an engaging and informal learning environment based on seminar-style classes and close collaboration between students and faculty. Delta College, the only program of its kind in the SUNY system, allows students to explore global issues through national and international study as part of an extensive experiential learning curriculum.

Recent and planned capital projects of Brockport include an $18 million town home development that houses 208 residents; a $6.5 million dining hall enhancement; a $40 million Special Events Recreation Center scheduled to be completed during the 2010–11 school year; a collaboration with the City of Rochester for the Lake Ontario Natural Resource Center; and a $30 million new academic building initiative—all designed to enhance the quality of the student experience at Brockport.

More than 30,000 alumni work and live in the Greater Rochester area. Many of the region's business leaders and entrepreneurs, teachers and nurses, scientists and scholars—drivers of social change and improved quality of life for all citizens—claim The College at Brockport as their alma mater and serve as ambassadors across the region and around the world. In keeping with its legacy, the college will continue to respond to the changing needs of its region, state, and country with an unwavering dedication to academic excellence and a commitment to student success.

Additional information about The College at Brockport, State University of New York (SUNY) can be found on the college's Web site at www.brockport.edu.

Far left: The Department of Art at Brockport offers a distinctive curriculum that integrates rigorous studio practice and advanced media technologies with liberal arts coursework. Center, top: Brockport Golden Eagles Athletics offers 23 intercollegiate sports teams, including lacrosse. Center, bottom: Brockport provides a first-rate education that blends modern technology with traditional tools and emphasizes small classes, individual instruction, and participation in research. Above: The Sankofa African Dance and Drum Ensemble of Brockport represents the rich cultural heritage that exists within the university community.

Monroe Community College

Considered one of the most innovative community colleges in North America, Monroe Community College is a leader in advanced technology, public safety, health care, and teacher education. MCC meets the community's needs for an educated workforce by providing classroom, online, and on-the-job education and training.

Above left: Monroe Community College (MCC) educates about 36,000 people from the Greater Rochester region each year. Above right: MCC students prepare for successful careers in the area's hot industries, including health care and optics.

For those who live in the Greater Rochester area, from high school graduates to adults at all stages in their lives and careers, a college education and advanced job training are not distant dreams. Monroe Community College (MCC) makes higher education accessible to a diverse community.

Each year, about 36,000 students enroll in the college's 85 degree and certificate programs. About a quarter of the area's recent high school graduates attend MCC. The college provides education and training that support industries critical to the local economy, including optical fabrication, advanced manufacturing, nursing, radiologic technology, agriculture, public safety, and teacher education.

At MCC, students aspiring to earn bachelor's degrees can complete their first two years here, then transfer to a four-year college or university. For those seeking shorter-term training, two-year programs prepare students for a specific technical or paraprofessional career. Certificate programs take less time.

Students engage in a variety of activities through more than 60 clubs and organizations. Leadership opportunities abound in these co-curricular activities and through a Leadership Institute that creates life-impacting experiences and prepares students for a successful future.

An indispensable and dynamic resource, MCC provides innovative solutions to the area's needs, stimulating and enriching the community. Its workforce offerings, which can be customized to client specifications, include business, health care, advanced manufacturing, and technical courses. In the 2006–07 school year, MCC trained workers at 727 companies and organizations.

MCC offers courses at its 300-acre Brighton Campus, its downtown Damon City Campus, its Applied Technologies Center, the Public Safety Training Facility, and community-based extension sites, as well as via the Internet. MCC is a leading provider of online courses in the State University of New York (SUNY) system.

Beyond its educational influence, the college has an economic impact locally of $704.7 million a year. In the 2006–07 academic year, the MCC Foundation raised about $7 million in private funds for students, faculty enrichment, and equipment, and more than $5.2 million in grants were brought into the community via MCC.

Since its first classes in 1962, MCC has educated nearly 400,000 students. By seeking new ways to meet the area's changing needs, the college continues to provide an educated, productive workforce. Additional information can be found on MCC's Web site at www.monroecc.edu.

6 5 4 3
3 4
kWh

PROFILES OF COMPANIES AND ORGANIZATIONS

Energy

Rochester Gas and Electric Corporation

A historic partner in community progress and economic development, this company today serves 360,000 electricity customers and 297,000 natural gas customers—helping to power the lives of people across the Rochester region as it has done for more than 150 years.

Above: By 1848, Rochester Gas Light Company—a predecessor of Rochester Gas and Electric Corporation (RG&E)—was manufacturing gas from coal and had installed gas mains and lamps, making Rochester the first city in upstate New York to have gas lamps.

For more than 150 years, Rochester Gas and Electric Corporation (RG&E) has provided essential energy to power the economy and the lives of people across the Rochester region. RG&E, however, is much more than an energy provider; the company's long tradition of supporting economic development and community activities makes RG&E an integral part of the fabric of the region.

A Continuing Tradition of Innovation

In 1848, not long after Rochester was incorporated as a town, Rochester Gas Light Company was manufacturing gas from coal and had installed gas mains and the first gas lamps in an upstate city. The company continued to grow and innovate with projects such as a 28-mile wooden natural gas pipeline from nearby production fields to Rochester. This pipeline was built to satisfy the growing demand for energy and to help keep prices low in the 1870s.

By 1879, the company brought electric light to Rochester. The Rochester Electric Light Company was founded a year later, but it was RG&E's direct predecessor, the Edison Electric Company, that was the first to install meters to measure electricity use and to put electric wires underground in downtown Rochester. These two electric companies and the Rochester Gas Light Company merged in 1892 to form RG&E. By 1919, the company served a region largely the same as its present nine-county area and RG&E's people were focused on providing outstanding customer service and safe, reliable electricity and natural gas service.

RG&E, a subsidiary of Energy East Corporation, now serves 360,000 electricity and 297,000 natural gas customers. Among these customers are more than 1,000 manufacturers, including Eastman Kodak Company, Xerox Corporation, and Bausch & Lomb Incorporated. These companies depend on RG&E for the competitive rates and reliable service that help them succeed in the global economy.

A Solid Commitment to the Environment

Beyond RG&E's continuing focus on customer service, safety, and reliability, the company has rededicated itself to environmental sustainability. The goal is to ensure that RG&E is able to meet today's needs without compromising the ability of future generations to meet the needs of tomorrow.

One of RG&E's most significant environmental accomplishments to date is a consistent and continuing reduction of carbon dioxide (CO_2) equivalent emissions. Since 1999, RG&E and the other Energy East utility companies have reduced their carbon footprint by 50 percent by cutting emissions of sulfur hexafluoride (SF_6), a nontoxic gas used as an insulator in substation equipment; by aggressively locating and repairing natural gas leaks to minimize methane emissions; by improving the fuel efficiency for fleet vehicles, in part by putting hybrid and partial zero emissions vehicles in service; and by increasing overall energy efficiency in buildings. Taken together, these CO_2 reductions are equivalent to planting more than 13 million trees or taking nearly 17,000 cars off the road.

RG&E is proud of two additional efforts to increase the region's supply of clean, renewable energy. First, the company is expanding two of its hydroelectric generating plants on the Genesee River in Rochester. Second, RG&E is pleased to offer—and proud that its customers enthusiastically support—the "Catch the Wind" program, which provides customers the opportunity to purchase wind energy. Customer participation in the wind energy program increased 70 percent from 2006 to 2007 and participants used nearly 34 million kilowatt hours of wind-generated electricity in 2007.

To build on this record of environmental sustainability, RG&E will continue to monitor and reduce its carbon footprint, engage its supply chain in supporting sustainable business practices, and initiate projects designed to achieve continuous improvements in operational efficiency.

A Strong Partner in Economic Development

The city of Rochester is at the heart of a region blessed with a highly educated workforce, a solid infrastructure, excellent educational systems, a high quality of life, and bountiful natural beauty. Working with economic development allies at the local, county, and state levels, RG&E helps to ensure that the region's many assets—as well as the rate and nonrate economic development funding programs the company offers—are part of the decision-making process of any business seeking to expand or relocate in the region.

Since 2004, RG&E's economic development team has provided approximately $50 million in direct grants and energy discounts to companies expanding or relocating in the Rochester region. Taken together, these grants and this assistance have been directly responsible for more than 8,000 new or retained jobs and more than $600 million in capital investment.

By continuing to provide outstanding customer service and safe, reliable energy delivery while meeting customers' energy requirements in an environmentally responsible manner, RG&E will continue to be a valuable asset to communities across the region. Additional information is available on RG&E's Web site at www.rge.com.

Left, top: RG&E is expanding two of its clean, renewable hydroelectric generating plants on the Genesee River in Rochester, including this one, Station 2 at High Falls. Left, bottom: RG&E ensures safe, reliable service to 360,000 electricity and 297,000 natural gas customers across nine counties. Center: RG&E has been lighting up the city and the region since Rochester was incorporated. Right: RG&E's "Catch the Wind" program promotes and provides wind energy.

PROFILES OF COMPANIES AND ORGANIZATIONS

Health Care and Medical Services & Facilities

Rochester General Hospital

This 528-bed, acute care tertiary hospital, a regional health care leader, offers an array of services including nationally recognized heart and cancer centers, a birthing center, and specialties in orthopaedics, women's health, primary care, and surgical, rehabilitative, pain management, behavioral health, and emergency services.

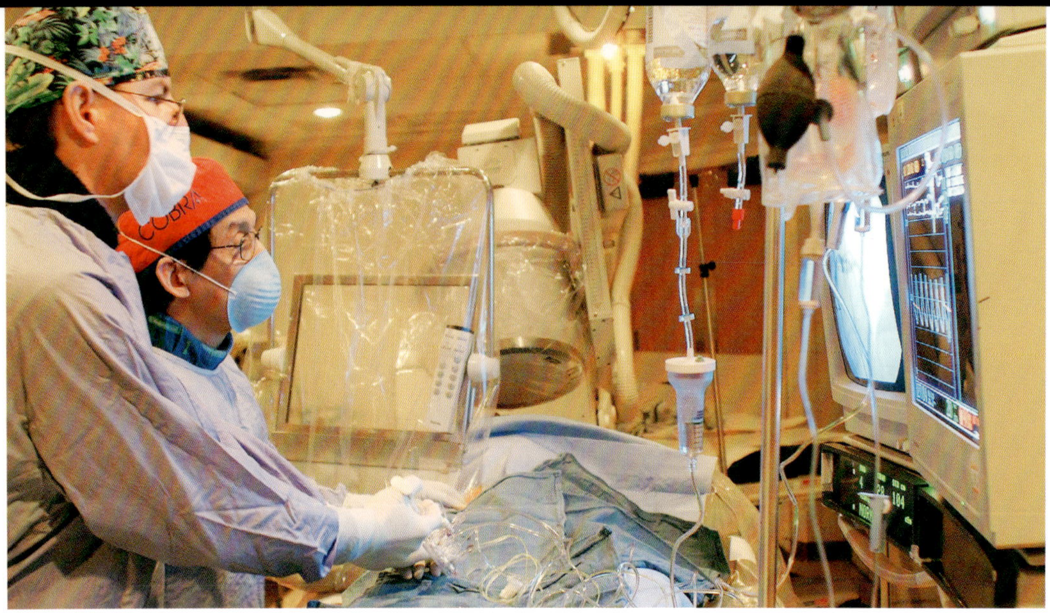

Above: The Cardiac Catheterization Laboratory consists of five state-of-the-art cardiac laboratories that perform more than 6,800 diagnostic and intervention procedures each year. Procedures performed in the laboratories include angioplasty, stent placement, and permanent pacemaker implantation.

For more than 160 years, Rochester General Hospital (RGH) has provided comprehensive, high quality care and service to residents of Greater Rochester and surrounding communities. In the process, it has evolved into a hospital that is nationally recognized for its clinical excellence and innovation, and has become a highly valued regional health care provider, routinely providing care to patients from the Finger Lakes and Southern Tier areas of New York state. At the same time, it serves more residents of Monroe County than any other hospital in the area.

RGH's services include a wide array of medical, obstetrical, pediatric, behavioral health, and surgical disciplines and specialties. The hospital provides inpatient and outpatient care as well as primary care delivered through a growing network of more than 40 multi-physician practices in Monroe and Wayne counties. Over the past decade alone, RGH has been independently recognized numerous times for excellence in clinical quality, as evidenced by these awards and designations:

- Solucient Top 100 Cardiovascular Hospital seven times, the only hospital in the region to receive this honor and one of only 20 hospitals nationwide to have achieved this distinction seven or more times
- Solucient Top 100 Performance Improvement Hospitals for improvements in both clinical and financial outcomes
- Premier Quality Award for Heart Attack Care and Quality Award for Cardiac Surgery as measured through clinical outcomes
- Named by *Money* magazine as one of the top 25 hospitals in heart care and hip surgeries
- Nurse Magnet accreditation, an honor which has been awarded to only 128 hospitals in the United States
- Gold Seal of Approval for the Stroke Center from the Joint Commission
- The region's only Teaching Hospital Cancer Program accredited by the American College of Surgeons
- The first hospital in New York state to receive the Baby Friendly designation from the World Health Organization and UNICEF

Building a Culture of Excellence

The physicians and staff at RGH have embraced the process of building a culture of excellence. A strong commitment to excellence every day exists with a goal of providing the very best patient experience possible. Recent improvements include, but are not limited to the following:

- Creating additional private rooms
- Providing free, flat-screen television service
- A unique menu of daily entree choices for patients
- Concierge service
- Long-term parking discounts

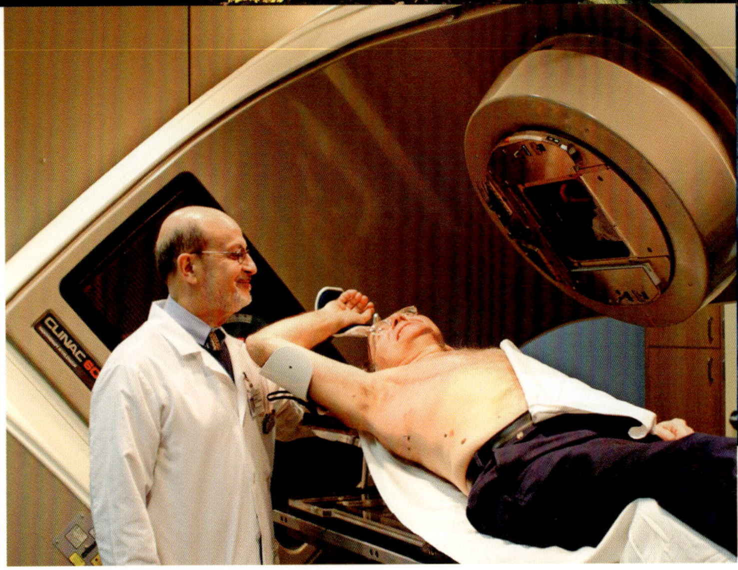

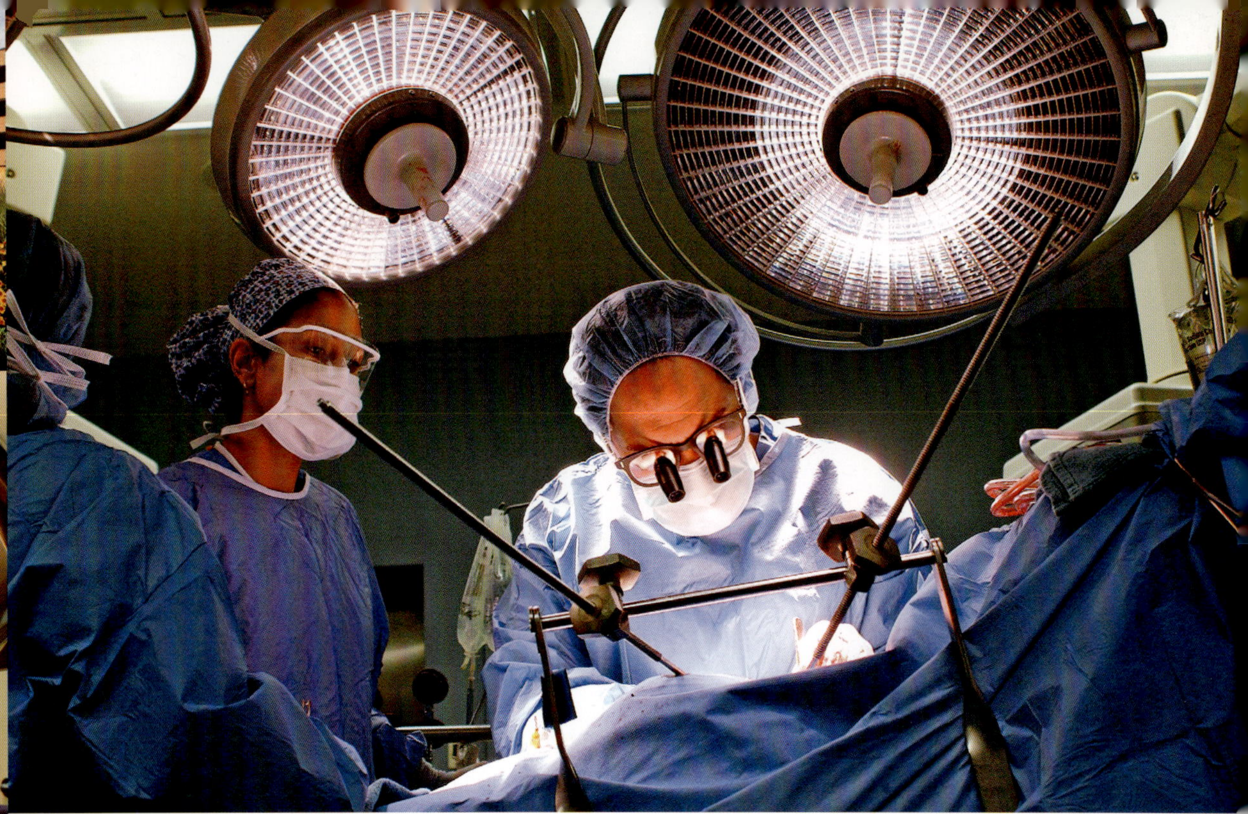

A Leader in Innovation and Technology

RGH physicians, administration, and staff maintain a sharp focus on bringing leading-edge technology home to Rochester to better care for the patients and families they serve. A prime example is RGH's investment in robotic surgery, a minimally invasive alternative which offers immense benefits to patients. The da Vinci Robotic Surgical System is utilized on an ever-increasing basis by urologists, cardiac surgeons, and general surgeons to perform robotic-assisted surgery. RGH was the first hospital in upstate New York to implement the da Vinci S HD Surgical System—the world's first robotic surgical system offering three-dimensional (3-D), high-definition vision. It provides surgeons twice the effective viewing resolution compared to other systems, which results in improved clarity and detail of tissue and critical anatomy. It enables surgeons at RGH to provide patients with new, minimally invasive surgical procedures that offer significant advantages over traditional "open" surgeries. These robotic-assisted, minimally invasive procedures—available to treat conditions as diverse as prostate cancer and hysterectomies—provide many benefits to patients, including less pain, discomfort, and blood loss, and a quicker return to normal activities.

RGH and its affiliates offer a Telehealth network, a component of an integrated plan designed to improve patient access to specialized services throughout Western New York, regardless of a patient's location. The Telehealth network is the first of its kind in the Greater Rochester region. It provides health care and consultative services to individual patients by using telecommunications technology to transmit information related to care over distances. RGH's TeleHealth program offers specialty physician consults to other hospitals and clinics in surrounding areas where recruitment of highly specialized physicians such as nephrologists; pulmonologists; vascular, plastic and bariatric surgeons; urologists; cardiologists; infectious disease specialists; and dermatologists has proven to be challenging.

Top left: Rochester General Hospital provides comprehensive health care services.
Below left: Radiation Oncology and Medical Physics offer complete radiation therapy services. The departments are equipped with two modern linear accelerators (one with electron capabilities) and an orthovoltage unit.
Above right: Doctors at the Rochester Heart Institute are leaders in cardiac surgery and treatments for all types of heart failure and disease.

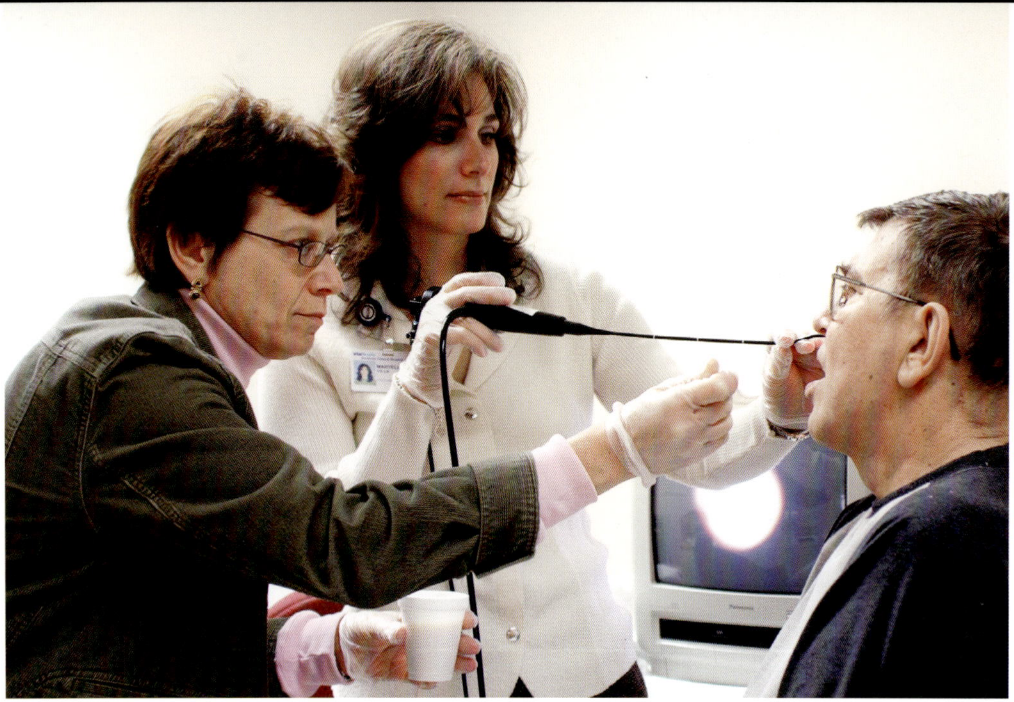

Above: Speech pathologists work with a patient to help him correct his speech and swallowing difficulties.

To enhance its diagnostic imaging capabilities, RGH recently installed a new 64-slice computed tomography (CT) scanner, one of the first in the Rochester area and the very first equipped with a software package that allows technicians to reduce and minimize radiation exposure to patients. In minutes, it can provide several dozen, high-definition images that will provide important improvements to both clinical diagnosis and care and patient convenience—and provide physicians with the most complete and accurate view they have ever had of their patients.

The Rochester Region's Recognized Leader in Cardiac Care

RGH is a leader in the region for heart care and has been named a Solucient Top 100 Heart Hospital seven times, a feat matched by just 19 other hospitals in the nation. Offering comprehensive cardiology and cardiovascular services, RGH is the fourth-largest cardiac surgery program (1,700 per year) in New York state.

The Rochester Heart Institute at RGH has a unique partnership with the Cleveland Clinic, named the number-one heart hospital in the nation by *U.S.News & World Report*. This partnership allows a sharing of expertise between physicians and surgeons at the two facilities and quicker access to leading-edge research and technology. RGH provides complete diagnostic services; medical, invasive, and noninvasive treatments; rehabilitation; and cardiothoracic surgery.

RGH also offers a state-of-the-art cardiac rehabilitation program through which patients receive counseling for diet and lifestyle changes, progressive exercise, and stress management following their cardiac event. Patients in cardiac rehabilitation are treated by a team of registered nurses and dieticians, exercise specialists, and social workers.

Innovation in Cancer Treatment

RGH's Lipson Cancer Center is committed to advancing cancer prevention, education, diagnosis, treatments, and research to provide patients with innovative therapy care for cancer and blood disorders. The center has a unique affiliation with Roswell Park Cancer Institute, and is highly involved in education and clinical research. RGH is the area's only Teaching Hospital Cancer Program accredited by the American College of Surgeons. Physicians and staff representing medical, radiation, and surgical oncology work together in a team approach to ensure the very best course of care for each and every patient.

The center offers a comfortable, private setting for patients and their families, including a patient lounge for those awaiting treatment, central chemotherapy, and radiation facilities, and an on-site phlebotomist to help reduce time spent going to other locations in the hospital complex for blood tests. A recently constructed satellite office at Linden Oaks Medical Campus provides comprehensive medical and radiation oncology services and is easily accessible for patients in southeast Monroe County.

A Wide Array of Services

The hospital's busy emergency department receives more than 85,000 visits each year, and a major expansion and renovation project will nearly double its size and further enhance the quality of care offered.

RGH offers patient and family-focused childbirth at the Twig Birthing Center. The hospital also provides comprehensive Women's Health Services with a homelike, in-hospital birthing center. The hospital provides diagnostic services for high-risk pregnancies with complete prenatal genetic testing and counseling. A special care nursery is available to care for most babies delivered at the hospital who have special needs. RGH's gynecologic surgical service provides the most up-to-date, minimally invasive, as well as more complicated gynecologic surgical procedures. RGH has achieved Baby Friendly designation from UNICEF and the World Health Organization.

Some outpatient services are provided at the former Genesee campus, now known as Alexander Park, including primary care for adults and children, allergy, asthma, and rheumatology services, along with the Diabetes Care and Resource Center. The Behavioral Health Network affiliated with RGH offers children and youth services treatment, adult outpatient services, older adult outpatient services, addiction recovery services, psychiatric rehabilitation services, and emergency and inpatient services.

Keeping an Eye on the Future

A modernization and expansion plan submitted to and approved by the New York State Department of Health in 2008 includes important improvements to the Portland Avenue campus that will further enhance the level of care offered to patients. The plan calls for a new six-story building connected to the south side of the hospital, additional private rooms, and the creation of an Ambulatory Services Pavilion that would provide a more convenient and accessible, centralized environment for ambulatory patients.

The plan represents Phase II of a long-range planning process initiated years ago and reflects RGH's commitment to providing the highest level of care and service for its patients. The plan is another logical step in that journey through which the exceptional medicine practiced at RGH will be matched by an environment that provides easy access, convenience, and comfort for those who entrust their care to RGH. Additional beds will also enable the hospital to provide a significantly greater percentage of private rooms—approximately 90 percent—a preference of the vast majority of patients.

The Highest Level of Nursing

RGH has earned the distinction of Nurse Magnet hospital, the nation's highest honor for daily nursing care excellence. To be considered, RGH was evaluated across 14 categories by the American Nursing Credentialing Center (ANCC). Magnet assessment teams also met with hospital staff, patients, volunteers, and board members. Its Magnet status signifies that Rochester General Hospital emphasizes the role of nursing as a key component of the overall hospital team. In addition to representing nursing excellence, Magnet status validates the dedication and commitment of the entire staff—physicians, pharmacists, therapists, service employees, volunteers, and organizational leaders—in making high quality patient care the number-one priority. More information about the hospital is available on its Web site at www.rochestergeneral.org.

Above: Rochester General Hospital has consistently received distinctions that reflect the quality care provided by a highly trained, dedicated staff.

Jewish Senior *Life*

Enriching and supporting the lives of seniors in Greater Rochester, Jewish Senior *Life*™ offers a continuum of senior living—from independent and enriched living apartments to skilled nursing care—as well as a host of community services that are characterized by respect, compassion, warmth, and dignity. Jewish Senior *Life* is Rochester's premier authority on healthy aging.

Above: Walking paths, fountains, gardens, and a tennis court adorn the beautiful 25-acre campus of Jewish Senior *Life*™.

Serving Rochester's seniors and their loved ones, Jewish Senior *Life*™ is dedicated to promoting healthy aging by creating environments that foster independence, further self-fulfillment, and achieve whole-person wellness. This organization provides a broad array of services and specialized programs to meet the needs of individuals who live on its campus as well as seniors who live in the greater community.

The roots of Jewish Senior *Life* go back to 1920, when five women began pursuing the creation of a Jewish nursing home in Rochester that would serve as a place for adults to age gracefully and with dignity. Their vision became a reality with the first Jewish Home, a large house on St. Paul Street that was home to seven full-time residents. Today Jewish Senior *Life* is more than solely a nursing home. It provides a full continuum of care on its 25-acre campus, located on Winton Road South, which encompasses the Summit at Brighton, for independent living; Wolk Manor, for enriched living; and the Jewish Home of Rochester. In addition, Jewish Senior *Life* has added community-based programs and services to enable people to live safely and comfortably in the location of their choice for as long as possible, whether that be on the Jewish Senior *Life* campus, in their own homes, in the home of a family member, or at any other location that they call home.

Open to people of all faiths and ethnic backgrounds, Jewish Senior *Life* bases its mission on its strong values of honoring mothers, fathers, and family; of emphasizing aging in place, which allows people to remain in the place of their choice; and of providing life care by offering a full continuum of care and a variety of health benefit plans that allow people to advance through the continuum without paying more for increased levels of care.

The Summit at Brighton

Residents at the Summit at Brighton enjoy first-class retirement living. The Summit's beautifully landscaped location includes walking trails, a tennis court, a putting green, a picnic area, ponds and fountains, and resident gardens. Indoors the Summit has a variety of spaces for residents' enjoyment as well, including several dining areas; a café; a cocktail lounge; a library; a fitness center; an indoor swimming pool and whirlpool spa; game rooms, which include billiards; and an art studio. The Summit's cultural arts program offers social, recreational, intellectual, and spiritual opportunities for residents, and the choice is always theirs as to whether they wish to participate.

The Summit also offers an array of services that free residents from everyday tasks and the responsibilities that come with owning a home. These services include flexible dining options, housekeeping and laundry services, routine maintenance and repair, scheduled courtesy transportation, and emergency response 24 hours a day. Residents also have priority access to Wolk Manor for assistance with daily living and the Jewish Home for transitional or long-term care.

The Summit at Brighton is Rochester's first and only life care community, offering a choice of health care benefit plans to help manage the cost of potential future long-term care. This allows residents freedom from worry about future and unforeseen medical expenses and peace of mind in knowing that they will receive quality health care for life, should it be needed.

Wolk Manor

For those who need day-to-day assistance, Wolk Manor combines comfortable apartment living with personal care services that deliver physical, mental, and emotional support to those who just need a little help to maintain an independent lifestyle. Licensed and trained caregivers develop close bonds with residents, whom they regard as family.

Wolk Manor residents have access to beautiful common areas for dining, entertainment, and socializing, including a variety of dining rooms, a country kitchen, television and sitting rooms, a beauty salon and barbershop, and numerous social activities that contribute to an engaging lifestyle. Assistance with daily activities; medication supervision; three daily nutritious meals; and an array of educational, cultural, and social opportunities help residents enjoy a high quality of life, while their families enjoy peace of mind. Respite stays are also available when caregivers need some time away and want to make sure that their loved one is safe and cared for in their absence.

The Jewish Home of Rochester

At the 362-bed Jewish Home of Rochester, full-time medical staff, geriatric nurse practitioners, and a highly trained nursing staff provide the finest in long-term care, transitional care, and memory care in an environment of warmth, respect, and appreciation for each resident's personal life experiences. The quality of life of residents and their families is of utmost importance; thus the philosophy of "family among families" is maintained.

The Jewish Home's residents enjoy upscale private and semiprivate rooms with flat-screen televisions, inviting restaurant-style dining, art therapy, music and activity programs, and wireless Internet access. For additional entertainment and convenience, the Street of Shops features a café, library, and computer center; a kosher delicatessen; a gift shop; a personal-banking center and ATM; and an enclosed porch with heated floors for year-round enjoyment.

Not only is the Jewish Home newly renovated with beautiful furnishings, but it is also privileged to have a large collection of artwork that adorns every hallway and public space for all to enjoy and appreciate.

Jewish Senior *Life Lines*

For those who prefer to live in their own homes for as long as possible, Jewish Senior *Life* provides *Life Lines*—programs and services designed to support seniors who live throughout the Rochester area. Outpatient Rehabilitation helps people regain their strength after an illness or injury to function safely and completely at home. At Home Services provides home repairs, housekeeping, lawn maintenance, and emergency-response system services. Physician House Calls brings specialists in geriatric care to the homes of older adults who have difficulty traveling to a doctor for care. Kosher2Go offers unique meal preparations for pickup or delivery. Adult Day Health Care and Home Health Care provide day and night care, companionship, and enrichment for area seniors. And the Jewish Hospice Program assists patients and families in making their loved one's remaining time meaningful and comfortable.

The variety of living options, programs, and services made available by Jewish Senior *Life* meets the needs of its residents and families; improves the health, well-being, and quality of life of Rochester's community of seniors; and sets the standard for quality care of older adults.

Jewish Senior *Life* provides additional information about the organization on its Web site at www.jewishseniorlife.org.

Above left: Jewish Senior *Life* features an extensive collection of original artwork throughout all areas of its campus. Above right: Jewish Senior *Life*'s Jewish Home of Rochester provides long-term, transitional, and memory care in a "family among families" culture.

Allergy Asthma Immunology of Rochester, P.C. (AAIR)

This private medical group specializes in providing quality care for children and adults who have allergic, rheumatologic, and immunologic diseases. The group is also dedicated to finding future treatments and to advancing the understanding of these conditions by conducting clinical and pharmaceutical research.

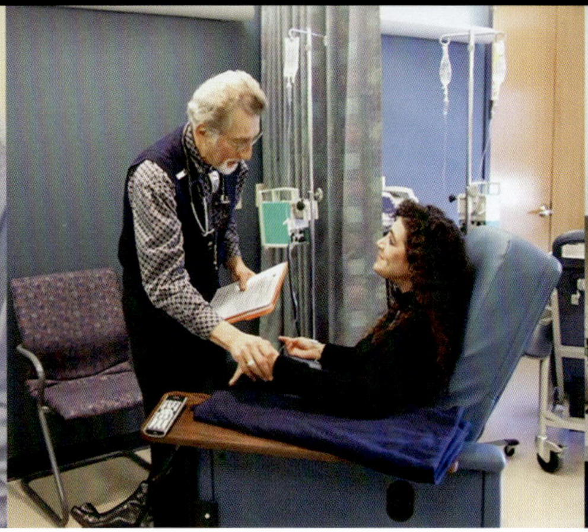

Above left: The partners of Allergy Asthma Immunology of Rochester, P.C. (AAIR) include, from right: Mariola B. Kubicka, M.D.; Albert S. Hartel, M.D.; Donald W. Pulver, M.D.; John J. Condemi, M.D.; Emmanuel A. Quaidoo, M.D.; and Peter M. G. Deane, M.D. All other photos: AAIR has been providing quality consultation and care of adults and children with asthma, allergies, and rheumatologic diseases since 1985. AAIR takes pride in offering advanced forms of diagnosis and treatment based on sound clinical investigations within its fields of specialization.

Allergy Asthma Immunology of Rochester, P.C. (AAIR) was founded in 1985 by John J. Condemi, M.D. and Robert H. Schwartz, M.D. AAIR has since grown into a nationally respected practice with physicians who are leaders in their fields. AAIR provides advanced diagnostic treatment options, such as rhinoscopy for evaluation of nasal and sinus symptoms, in four convenient state-of-the-art facilities. AAIR's on-site infusion center, overseen by a physician and a registered nurse, treats patients with arthritis, psoriasis, ulcerative colitis, Crohn's disease, and osteoporosis.

AAIR serves as a teaching facility for doctors and other medical professionals in training. It has an annual education seminar for doctors, nurses, and child care providers. AAIR doctors are often quoted as experts on local radio and television and in newspapers. AAIR physicians are all board certified, hold academic appointments at the University of Rochester Medical Center, and have privileges at several area hospitals. Some have been included in the *Best Doctors in America* and have received national and local awards. The medical staff is active in academic circles, presenting expert talks, writing journal articles and book chapters, and sharing their knowledge with others by attending regional and national meetings.

AAIR has one of the largest practice-based sites in the United States for pharmaceutical-sponsored research. For decades the group's experienced physicians and staff have conducted clinical trials—controlled, FDA-approved scientific studies to determine if investigational medications are safe and effective. Rochester residents are recruited to participate in AAIR studies in order to help themselves and others, while obtaining some of the most promising medications to treat allergic, rheumatic, and lung diseases. Most of the drugs used for these diseases today were studied at AAIR.

AAIR research not only contributes to the health of the greater Rochester community but also brings more than 30 individuals per month from out of the state to the site. These individuals help to stimulate the local economy through car rentals, restaurant dining, and stays at hotels.

AAIR has been and continues to be a leader in the field of allergy, immunology, rheumatology, and clinical research and is committed to improving the current and future health of the Rochester and Finger Lakes communities.

Elizabeth Wende Breast Care, LLC

This breast imaging and breast disease diagnosis center is ranked as one of the nation's leading breast care facilities. It provides mammography, digital mammography, breast MRI, breast ultrasound, stereotactic breast biopsy, dexa scan, and computer-aided detection (CAD) in reading mammograms.

Elizabeth Wende Breast Care, LLC (EWBC) is internationally recognized as a leader in the field of breast imaging and breast cancer diagnosis. It is one of the largest freestanding breast imaging centers in the United States, and is the largest single-site breast imaging center in New York State. EWBC has been designated as a Breast Imaging Center of Excellence by the American College of Radiology (ACR).

Since its inception in 1975, the mission of EWBC has been to provide high quality imaging and patient care, even when it meant breaking the mold of the traditional radiology practice. As one of the true pioneers of modern breast imaging, Dr. Wende Logan-Young's entrepreneurial spirit, intense dedication, and passion for the field resulted not only in a thriving practice, but also in many of the technical and procedural improvements that are considered standards of care in the United States today.

Today, EWBC is a group practice of five breast imaging specialists—Dr. Stamatia Destounis, Dr. Philip Murphy, Dr. Patricia Somerville, Dr. Wende Logan-Young, and Dr. Posy Seifert, who has been the group's managing partner since 2005. They handle the needs of more than 150,000 patients and continue to break the mold by instituting and participating in innovative research studies. The physicians of EWBC regularly present their research and lecture at major medical meetings around the world.

With major technical advancements being made in the field, the patient volume and size of EWBC have made the practice an attractive clinical study setting for manufacturers of breast imaging modalities and accessories. EWBC has participated with the American College of Radiology Imaging Network (ACRIN) in several breast imaging studies, including the Digital Mammography Imaging Screening Trial (DMIST), which compared the efficacy of full-field digital mammography with film and screen mammography, and the magnetic resonance imaging (MRI) evaluation of the contralateral breast in women with a recent diagnosis of breast cancer. Most recently, EWBC is performing a clinical study with Koning Corp., located in Rochester, to evaluate the new technology of coned breast computed tomography (CT).

Throughout the years and the many advances seen in the technology of breast imaging, the mission of Elizabeth Wende Breast Care, LLC has remained the same—to provide patients with excellent care that considers both their physical and emotional well-being. Elizabeth Wende Breast Care, LLC is deeply involved in community breast cancer awareness events and patient advocacy. Additional information about Elizabeth Wende Breast Care, LLC can be found on the company's Web site at www.ewbc.com.

Above left: Elizabeth Wende Breast Care, LLC (EWBC) is located in Rochester, New York. Above right: EWBC's five breast imaging specialists have extensive experience in breast MRI, breast ultrasound, image-guided breast biopsy, computer-aided detection, and breast disease detection and diagnosis. They also take part in groundbreaking research studies and share their research data at medical conferences.

PROFILES OF COMPANIES AND ORGANIZATIONS

Insurance Services

Preferred Care and MVP Health Care

This health care plan—in partnership with expert clinical care providers—develops high quality, cost-effective health plans that are designed to improve health care delivery, to exceed customers' expectations, and to help all members improve their health. Together, Preferred Care and MVP Health Care serve more than 700,000 members throughout New York State, Vermont, and New Hampshire.

Above: Preferred Care encourages its members to get healthy and stay healthy.

After almost three decades in business, Preferred Care and its parent company—MVP Health Care—remain determined as ever to help the communities they serve take on life and live well.

Preferred Care and MVP Health Care's membership continues to build—this network now provides health insurance solutions for 15,000 employers; serves more than 700,000 members throughout New York State, Vermont, and New Hampshire; and is powered by the ideas and energy of more than 1,700 employees. Preferred Care's plan options are also growing. From its new suite of personal choice and lifestyle plans to its top-rated health maintenance organization (HMO) plans to its lower-cost plans that offer total control, Preferred Care innovates new ways to meet and anticipate the needs of today's businesses.

Preferred Care's growth, success, and many innovations—all driven by its fundamental commitment to satisfy the needs of the people, businesses, and communities it serves—provide peace of mind in an increasingly complex environment. Today, that commitment is stronger than ever for Preferred Care.

Leading the Way

Anticipating the market demand for more options and positioning the company to compete with large, national health insurance providers, Preferred Care, with MVP Health Care, has broadened its product offerings beyond its HMO to include such options as individual insurance and personalized plans.

Since Preferred Care and MVP Health Care combined in 2006, the health plan strengthened its expertise in Medicare—allowing it to bring wellness-oriented care to a growing population of older adults. Among the top-rated health plans in the nation, Preferred Care and MVP Health Care continue to raise the bar for quality and customer service, as this health plan constantly seeks new ways to improve the processes and practices of health care.

Stable and Strong

In the highly competitive health insurance industry, Preferred Care and MVP Health Care have earned a reputation for financial stability. The Weiss Rating Service recently upgraded MVP Health Care's financial status to "A," or excellent. Preferred Care and MVP Health Care are proud of that distinction, which recognizes the health plan's solid foundation as it continues to grow.

Expanding Options: Solutions for All

Preferred Care and MVP Health Care have products designed to meet the needs of businesses large and small. The network pioneered HMO plans over two decades ago in order to give organizations the ability to provide high quality health insurance at an affordable cost. Since then, the network has expanded its range of products, delivering the flexibility that employers need to satisfy

their employees. Working closely with employers, this network continues to develop the new products that businesses need.

Today, Preferred Care and MVP Health Care can tailor a solution for any organization, from a family business around the corner to a major corporation with employees across the country. Working closely with employers, the network continues to develop the new products that businesses need, without sacrificing high standards of quality and customer service. Preferred Care and MVP Health Care's service highlights include

- **Prevention/Disease Management**—featuring a wide range of helpful programs such as disease management for diabetes and asthma; wellness programs for expectant mothers; and support programs, including smoking cessation;
- **'Work Well, Live Well'**—its proprietary worksite wellness program that encourages employees to take charge of their health, thereby optimizing physical and mental wellness through activities and programs, and offers potential benefits for employers, including reduced absenteeism, greater productivity, and happier, healthier employees;
- **National Network**—through a strategic alliance with CIGNA HealthCare, Preferred Care and MVP Health Care can cover members who reside or travel outside its service area with a national provider network of more than 500,000 doctors, hospitals, and specialists located across the country.

Improving Quality: Always Better

The MVP Health Care family is driven by a belief that health care can always be better—in customer service, in clinical excellence, and in flexibility. This network constantly works to improve communication with employers, members, and health care providers at every point of contact. It uses the most advanced technologies to simplify access to information and to streamline the process of health insurance. Overall, it serves more than 700,000 members and is always committed to quality service.

The MVP Health Care family also believes that all health care is local and personal—that the relationship between the doctor and the patient is where good medicine begins. Therefore, the network is dedicated to maintaining stable, long-term relationships with physicians and health care providers. It depends on providers to take great care of its members—and it fully supports them in this mission.

Honored for Superior Performance

For the commitment to quality care and responsive service, Preferred Care and MVP Health Care have received local and national recognition. The National Committee for Quality Assurance (NCQA), an independent, nonprofit organization dedicated to improving the quality of health care delivered to people everywhere, has rated both Preferred Care and MVP Health Care "Excellent" for the network's commercial health plans.

In a listing of "America's Best Health Plans 2007" from *U.S.News & World Report* and NCQA, Preferred Care and MVP Health Care health plans were among the top ranked in the nation for the third consecutive year. Preferred Care Gold, a Medicare Advantage health plan, is the highest-ranked Medicare plan in New York State and is number four in the nation.

In an industry that continually changes, Preferred Care and MVP Health Care are known for providing superior health care and customer service at the lowest possible cost. The organization's commitment to making health care simple and easy continues to empower members, giving them the information and services to experience healthier living.

Additional information about Preferred Care can be found on the health plan's Web site at www.preferredcare.org.

Above, both photos: Through personal guidance, complete support, and a true commitment to wellness, Preferred Care employees help members meet their own individual needs, goals, and challenges so they can make the most of every day.

PROFILES OF COMPANIES AND ORGANIZATIONS

Manufacturing and Distribution

Bausch & Lomb

This world-famous eye-health company—dedicated to 'perfecting vision and enhancing life'—develops some of the most familiar and highly regarded eye care brands in the world. With a commitment to innovation, Bausch & Lomb invents materials, develops technologies, and pioneers new ways to help people see better.

Right: Bausch & Lomb (B&L) was founded in 1853. Its world headquarters is located in Rochester, New York.

Bausch & Lomb (B&L) is an eye-health company whose goal and promise is to enhance the quality of people's lives worldwide through improved vision. Its portfolio of vision care, prescription and over-the-counter pharmaceuticals, and surgical products includes soft and rigid gas-permeable contact lenses, lens care solutions, ophthalmic surgical equipment, and ophthalmic drugs. Headquartered in Rochester, New York, and employing approximately 13,000 people worldwide, it is among the largest global providers of eye care products, with products available in more than 100 countries.

A Historic Partner in Progress

The B&L story began when two German immigrants, John Jacob ("J. J.") Bausch and Henry Lomb, arrived in America separately in 1849 and became friends after settling in Rochester. In 1853 Bausch opened a small optical goods shop—a business that was founded on the idea of selling superior eyeglass lenses and frames, a $60 loan from Lomb, and a handshake. Lomb helped keep the shop open by making small loans, even while he served with the 13th New York Volunteers in the Union army during the Civil War. Once Lomb had returned safely home to Rochester, Bausch made him a partner in the business, which then became the Bausch & Lomb Optical Company. The company's innovative eyeglass frames of vulcanized rubber were such a success that the partners were able to open a sales office in New York City in 1866, then eventually to pass a thriving business into the care of Bausch's sons, Edward and William.

Edward and William Bausch continued their father's and his partner's tradition of innovation as they led the company from the Gilded Age into the streamlined world of the 20th century. The company was incorporated in 1908, and in 1915 it produced the first optical-quality glass made in America. It then supplied the military during World War I with lenses for binoculars, periscopes, and searchlights. In the 1930s B&L brought out glare-reducing sunglasses for the United States Army Air Corps that, as the Ray-Ban line, was an important part of the B&L portfolio until 1999, when it was sold to Italian eyewear giant Luxottica.

In 2006 B&L completed its new R&D Center—a $35 million, 75,000-square-foot research, development, and engineering facility that is a wing of the B&L Optics Center in Rochester. The complex is the working home of more than 200 scientists, engineers, and support staff, plus hundreds more manufacturing, marketing, sales, and operations employees. B&L also has other facilities across the country as well as in Europe and the Asia-Pacific region. The company makes available additional information about its activities and products on its Web site (www.bausch.com).

In 1952 B&L produced the CinemaScope lens, delivering wide-screen effects with a single projector, for which it won an Oscar in 1955.

The business that two friends had founded on an idea and a small loan grew to become a major producer of microscopes, binoculars, projectors, and camera lenses and shutters. Mainstay products developed and introduced by the company include the first soft contact lens, in the early 1970s, and the first all-in-one cleaning, disinfecting, and storage solution for contact lenses, in the mid 1980s. In the 1990s B&L launched its next generation of contact lenses, including the PureVision, SofLens66 Toric, and SofLens Multi-Focal brands.

An Industry and Technology Leader

Today, with an eye-health market that has grown to be worth billions of dollars, B&L's product sectors—contact lenses and lens care products; pharmaceuticals; and opthalmic microsurgery products and refractive surgery systems—have made the company a global force in the ophthalmic industry. Among the products of these businesses are ocular vitamins, eye drops, and systems for rapidly and safely removing cataracts and replacing them with artificial lenses.

A Community Contributor

B&L invests in its community in many ways, including making substantial contributions to the University of Rochester. B&L works with the Rochester Institute of Technology for microsystems engineering research and the University of Rochester's Eye Institute, a collaboration that, among other benefits, has brought a dramatic increase in the number of eye doctors in Greater Rochester who treat complex visual problems. In an effort to mobilize the resources of governments, care-giving organizations, and industry to prevent blindness, B&L has donated $1 million and joined with the International Agency for the Prevention of Blindness and also Vision 2020–The Right to Sight, which works with the World Health Organization to eliminate the main causes of avoidable blindness by 2020.

In 2007 B&L was acquired by global private equity firm Warburg Pincus in a deal worth approximately $4.5 billion. The company that J. J. Bausch and Henry Lomb founded long ago remains focused on the business priorities and philosophies of its founders. B&L continues its work on the frontiers of eye health to prevent, treat, and perhaps even cure eye diseases. The company holds that its success arises from the efforts of its employees, its research partners and customers, and its communities.

Above left: In the 1970s B&L created the world's first soft contact lens. Above right: In 2006 the company opened its new Bausch & Lomb R&D Center, a state-of-the-art, 75,000-square-foot research, development, and engineering facility adjacent to the B&L Optics Center in Rochester.

Harris Corporation

Harris Corporation is a leading supplier of secure voice and data communications products, systems, and networks to military, government, and commercial organizations worldwide. Its Harris RF Communications Division business unit was built from humble beginnings and has grown into an international communications corporation renowned for its best-in-class secure radio products.

Operating out of a Park Avenue basement in 1960, four local businessmen started a company called RF Communications to satisfy an emerging market for communications via long-distance radios. In 1969, RF Communications merged with Harris-Intertype Corporation of Melbourne, Florida, to become Harris RF Communications Division (Harris RFCD).

Before "globalization" became a buzzword, Harris RFCD was, in essence, a global company. One of the start-up company's first targets was underdeveloped countries with unreliable long-distance telephone systems. Today, the RF Communications Division of Harris Corporation has supplied government and commercial customers in more than 150 countries with its best-in-class communications equipment and unparalleled customer support.

In addition to secure radio products and systems, the company designs and manufactures state-of-the-art military networking products, sensors, software, antennas, radio accessories, and custom-built systems. Its embedded encryption modules are recognized by the U.S. government as the gold standard. Over the past decade, Harris RFCD's dedication to delivering value and innovation to its customers has earned the company many government agency certifications for technological product advancements and industry certifications for excellence in manufacturing processes.

Although Harris RFCD has expanded far beyond the Park Avenue basement—with more than 2,200 employees in Rochester and also with facilities in Maryland, Florida, California, and the United Kingdom—the values shared by its four founders are still the core of the company: innovation, entrepreneurial spirit, teamwork, and a connection to the customer and company mission. Harris RFCD has a culture of excellence where innovation is a catalyst for change, technology is pervasive, growth is enabled by challenging the status quo, and most importantly, where the right group of talented people makes all the difference.

Employees of Harris RFCD drive growth and innovation not only at work, but also in the community. Transferring the company value of teamwork into community involvement, employees donate their time and financial support to several Rochester organizations and participate in events such as the American Heart Association Heart Walk, Habitat for Humanity, and the JPMorgan Chase Corporate Challenge. Various local charities—including the Veterans Outreach Center, Greater Rochester Chapter of the American Red Cross, Fallen Soldiers, and Special Olympics—receive financial contributions from Harris RFCD.

To encourage a future supply of engineers and scientists, employees are involved in a variety of educational activities for local students. The company hosts tours of its manufacturing facilities for high school groups, including science and math programs associated with the Rochester City School District. Employees are frequent guest speakers at local schools, discussing engineering and technology-related careers. High school students work with Harris RFCD

mentors throughout the year on the F.I.R.S.T. (For Inspiration and Recognition of Science and Technology) robotics team to design and build task-oriented robots for regional, national, and international competitions.

At the collegiate level, Harris RFCD maintains strong ties to local universities such as the University of Rochester and Rochester Institute of Technology (RIT). Many Harris RFCD employees are alumni of or currently enrolled at the University of Rochester's Simon Graduate School of Business. Harris RFCD is one of the top national employers of graduates from RIT's Kate Gleason College of Engineering, and in 2007, the company financed the Harris Corporation Computer Engineering Design Center, a collaborative resource area where project teams design and develop prototype solutions. RIT's "WE@RIT" Women in Engineering organization, which offers mentoring and outreach programs for young women pursuing careers in engineering, has also benefited from Harris RFCD sponsorship, co-hosting academic forums and career fairs with the company.

Through its robust co-op and internship program, Harris RFCD maintains strong relationships with several academic institutions outside of the Rochester area, offering students from universities across the country the opportunity to work on project teams at Harris RFCD. CollegeGrad.com, a leading entry-level job posting Web site, named Harris Corporation to its list of "Top Intern Employers."

As the company looks to the future and continues to expand its markets and global presence, it will also continue to expand opportunities for its people. Whether joining the Harris RFCD family as a new college graduate or a seasoned expert, Harris RF Communications Division of Harris Corporation is a place where everyone is a part of a dynamic team that quickly responds to the challenges faced by customers, the entrepreneurial spirit is the fuel for change, and all contributions can flourish in a stimulating environment rich in opportunity for innovation and discovery. More information about the company is available on its Web site at www.rfcomm.harris.com.

Harris RF Communications Division—a business unit of Harris Corporation—is dedicated to delivering assured communications. This page, left: Harris RFCD's ISO-9001:2000 and CMMI Level 3 certified manufacturing facilities build and test an average of 10,000 radios each month. This page, center: Ed Maier, Harris RFCD's vice president/general manager of Engineering and Operations, is shown with Penfield High School students from the F.I.R.S.T. robotics team. This page, right: Forming International Government Systems with a sister division, Harris RFCD aims to create a one-stop shop for international customers. Opposite page: Harris employees demonstrate the AN/PRC-117G radio.

Xerox Corporation

Specializing in desktop printers, multifunction office systems, high-speed color presses, outsourcing, and digital imaging, this document-management company offers the industry's broadest portfolio of document systems and services to accommodate business of any size. The company's operations are guided by customer-focused and employee-centered values such as environmental sustainability, citizenship, diversity, and quality.

Above left: A Xerox science consultant demonstrates a science experiment with Rochester City School District elementary students. Above right: Rochester is home to more than 7,000 Xerox employees.

Originally named The Haloid Company, Xerox Corporation was founded in 1906 to manufacture photographic paper and equipment. Half a decade later, in 1959, the company established itself as an industry leader by introducing the first plain-paper, automatic photocopier using the process of xerography developed by Chester Carlson in 1938. A string of successful products followed: the first desktop copier in 1963, the first wide-format engineering copier in 1979, and the DocuTech Production Publisher Model 135 in 1990.

Today the name Xerox has become synonymous with the process of photocopying, making the company a household name and an office staple. With sales of $17 billion, Xerox is the world's largest technology and services company specializing in document management.

Although Xerox headquarters are in Norwalk, Connecticut, the largest concentration of its U.S. employees—23 percent—are located in Monroe County, New York. Rochester is home to more than 7,000 Xerox employees who work in the company's research, engineering, manufacturing, assembly, sales, and marketing operations. Nearby Webster, New York, is another company hub that serves as the location of the Xerox Research Center, the Xerox Innovation Group, the Gil Hatch Center for Customer Innovation, and the Xerox iGen Customer Training Center.

The company's economic investment, philanthropic giving, and volunteer support within Rochester have always been substantial. During the last decade, Xerox contributed more than $25 million to the area's educational, cultural, and community organizations. Employee volunteerism and in-house programs also benefit the region: Social Service Leave, Xerox Community Involvement Program, Xerox Science Consultant Program, and the FIRST Robotics program.

The company's economic impact on Greater Rochester is sizable: $831 million in payroll; $4.5 million in property taxes; $504 million spent with local suppliers; and $93 million for investments in new facilities and upgrades since 2000. Millions more have been donated to the Rochester Institute of Technology, Monroe Community College, and the University of Rochester.

The Xerox Foundation provides $1 million every year to the United Way of Greater Rochester. Employees and retirees donate another million and more than 1,600 employees participate in the annual United Way Day of Caring. With a strong presence in the community and a commitment to outstanding corporate citizenship, Xerox Corporation plans to continue its tradition of forging long-lasting relationships that strengthen the community. More information about the company is provided on its Web site at www.xerox.com.

Gleason Corporation

'Keeping the World in Motion™,' this company is a global leader in gear production technology. It features the industry's most complete array of gear solutions for products used in the air, in space, at sea, and on land—from the largest wind power turbines to new eight-speed automobile transmissions to power tools.

Since 1865, Gleason Corporation has pioneered the development of the machines, tooling, processes, services, and technologies that are needed to produce bevel and cylindrical gears found virtually everywhere—from automobiles and airplanes to trucks and tractors, from giant wind turbines that can power a thousand homes to the lawn mowers and power tools found at these homes.

Today the global need for quieter, stronger, more affordable gears has never been greater, or the stakes higher. The explosive growth of developing countries, such as China and India, and an insatiable global demand for everything from materials and energy to farmland and roads have helped fueled an unprecedented demand for advanced gear production technology.

Many industries and companies find the solutions at Gleason. With customers on nearly every continent and locations in more than 25 countries, Gleason stands alone in its ability to deliver "total solutions" to solve customers' challenges anywhere in the world. Gleason is the only company that can offer solutions for the production and inspection of the complete range of gear types and sizes.

The production and inspection of these products involve gear and pinion cutting and grinding machines, tooling, and testers of the bevel gear sets that are used in the transmissions of vehicles as diverse as Hummers and Mercedes-Benzes. These cylindrical gear cutting and grinding machines—and the cutting tools and grinding wheels they use—also produce gears that are several meters in diameter for use in massive mining equipment weighing hundreds of tons as well as wind turbines that are taller than the Statue of Liberty.

Gleason's strategy of investing in the development of advanced technologies that are many times more productive than what was possible just a few years ago has helped double its global sales in the last three years alone. Technology, however, is not the only focus. Gleason also leads in its investment in the manufacturing, service, and support infrastructure and in the worldwide presence that is needed to respond to the new global manufacturing landscape.

This page, right: Worldwide headquarters for Gleason Corporation, along with major manufacturing operations, are based in Rochester, New York. Additional manufacturing, sales, and service facilities are strategically located throughout North and South America, Europe, and the Asia-Pacific region. Opposite page, both images: Gleason's new two-meter cell is used for the production of large gears for wind power applications.

Gleason's worldwide corporate headquarters and manufacturing operations are based in Rochester, New York. Additional manufacturing facilities are strategically located in Rockford, Illinois, and in Dayton, Ohio, as well as in Plymouth, England; Munich and Ludwigsburg, Germany; Bangalore, India; Studen, Switzerland; and Suzhou, China. Additional sales and service offices are located throughout North and South America, Europe, and the Asia-Pacific region.

Gleason Corporation is always moving forward—and always "Keeping the World in Motion™." Additional information can be found on Gleason Corporation's Web site at www.gleason.com.

Gleason-PFAUTER
P 2000 G
Gleason-PFAUTER
P 2000

Eastman Kodak Company

An iconic brand that has been synonymous with photography and imaging since 1888, Eastman Kodak Company is the world's foremost imaging innovator. From consumer products to film and entertainment to graphic communications, Kodak helps people and businesses make, manage, and move images and information, bringing Kodak moments everywhere to life.

Above left: George Eastman's (left) introduction of the first commercial transparent roll film in 1889 enabled inventor Thomas Edison (right) to develop the first motion picture camera in 1891; by 1896 Kodak was marketing film for motion picture use. Above right: Made in Rochester, KODAK NEXPRESS Digital Presses help commercial printers grow their business through applications like personalized direct mail and photo books. Opposite page: Image sensors from Kodak provide outstanding performance, resolution, and image quality.

It is hard to imagine Greater Rochester without Eastman Kodak Company's innovations and its commitment to strengthening the community's social, cultural, and educational tapestry. George Eastman founded Kodak with a simple promise: "You press the button, we do the rest." In addition, his philanthropy helped create United Way of Greater Rochester and fuel arts and education organizations across the region. Today Kodak is building upon its historic tradition of commitment to the community.

Kodak has been a world leader in imaging for more than 120 years. Whether helping people capture and share their memories, helping filmmakers bring stories to life, or helping businesses grow through print innovation, Kodak delivers imaging products and services that matter.

Kodak recognizes and values its strongest asset—its employees. By day, they are innovators and brand champions. Outside the workplace, they serve as volunteers, mentors, and change agents for not-for-profit agencies. Together with its employees, in 2008 Kodak committed cash contributions, in-kind support, and on-site volunteer participation in the Rochester Chapter of the Red Cross Fire & Ice event; the Wegmans LPGA Golf Tournament; the Junior League of Rochester's 75th Anniversary celebration; and the Clarissa Street Reunion, among many other local and national activities. Members of Kodak's eight employee networks helped organize and drive outreach activities at public schools in the area, supported the new Rochester Native American Film Festival, and contributed to other programs that support diversity and education.

On a broader scale, Kodak and its employees combined in 2008 to again make the largest contribution to the annual campaign of United Way of Greater Rochester and the American Red Cross Greater Rochester Chapter. The company also made a multimillion-dollar commitment in 2008 to the University of Rochester, Eastman Theatre, and Rochester Philharmonic Orchestra. Kodak is a founding sponsor of the WeROC campaign and also donated hundreds of thousands of dollars in goods, equipment, and materials across the region to schools, universities, and agencies that help keep Rochester a thriving, exciting place in which to live and work.

Kodak's technological innovations are legendary. The company made photography "as convenient as the pencil" in the late 1880s, and invented the first working digital camera prototype in 1975. Today Kodak innovations are making inkjet printing more affordable, detecting counterfeit goods, creating organic light-emitting displays, advancing next-generation sensors for digital cameras, and more. Additional information is available on the company's Web sites at www.kodak.com and at www.kodak.com/go/followus.

With all of its innovations and more to come, Kodak is helping consumers, businesses, and creative professionals unleash the power of pictures and printing to enrich their lives.

Kodak

PROFILES OF COMPANIES AND ORGANIZATIONS

Philanthropic Organizations and Nonprofits

Dixon Schwabl

Established in 1987 in Rochester, New York, Dixon Schwabl provides marketing communications services to 150 clients and philanthropic support to dozens of not-for-profit organizations. Dixon Schwabl has been recognized by the Great Place to Work® Institute and the Society for Human Resource Management as one of the Best Small Companies to Work for in America for the past four years, ranking number one in 2008.

Above right: Dixon Schwabl and its team of 75 employees serve not-for-profit organizations across the Rochester, New York, area by donating thousands of hours annually, including helping the Rochester City Ballet with public relations and fund-raising initiatives throughout the year.

Rochester has a strong history of giving back to the community, frequently ranking among the five top cities in the nation for per capita contributions to not-for-profit organizations. With its strong tradition of entrepreneurial activity and goodwill, Rochester has historically embraced innovative approaches to philanthropy.

Rochester's 'WOW' Community: A Legacy of Giving Back

From George Eastman's earliest days in the late 1800s and early 1900s to the creativity and inspiration of the Horses on Parade program in 2001, Rochester's not-for-profits receive outstanding support from business leaders in the area—including Dixon Schwabl.

Dedicating time and energy to not-for-profits is a way to strengthen the Rochester community, improving the lives of those who live and work in the region.

Dixon Schwabl enjoys the energy and excitement of working on philanthropic projects such as Horses on Parade, a community-wide fiberglass-animal parade created in partnership with High Falls Brewing Company and considered to be the largest fund-raising event in Rochester history. The team at Dixon Schwabl has developed and implemented innovative philanthropic efforts for dozens of clients. Its efforts include charitable galas and events, coffee-table books, and groundbreaking interactive-giving programs. More than a half-dozen books have been developed for charitable purposes, including *Horses on Parade*, as well as a series of books featuring spectacular or unique homes in the Rochester and Finger Lakes regions, and celebrity cookbooks. One hundred percent of the proceeds from these books benefit not-for-profits in the area, including groups dedicated to helping urban youth who are at risk and children who have learning disabilities.

Throughout its 20-year history, Dixon Schwabl has donated more than $11 million in time and services to philanthropic organizations. One hundred percent of the firm's 75 employees volunteer in some capacity for not-for-profit organizations in the area.

Dixon Schwabl is known for its dedication to not-for-profits and its commitment to volunteerism, with many of its employees and principals participating on boards, co-chairing galas, and helping at community events throughout the year. From golf tournaments to black-tie galas, employees provide an array of philanthropic support in Rochester year-round. Rochester's fine arts and performing arts groups are world renowned, with Garth Fagan Dance, Rochester City Ballet, and the Rochester Philharmonic Orchestra among the organizations benefiting from philanthropic support. Rochester's educational initiatives, such as EnCompass Resources for Learning and Hillside Work-Scholarship Connection, are models for the nation, helping students

to maximize their strengths and make the most of their educational opportunities. Humanitarian causes receive significant funds from concerned leaders in the area. Visiting Nurse Service Meals on Wheels delivers nutritious, complete meals to members of the community to ensure that they can enjoy a healthy and warm meal in the comfort of their own home. At home or out in the community, Dixon Schwabl's generous support is given where it is needed, when it is needed.

Dixon Schwabl also believes in empowering employees to develop their own areas of support for not-for-profits. Each year employees are given a "Make It Happen" day to support the cause of their choice by taking a paid day off to donate time to a not-for-profit and to report on their activities to their co-workers. This inspires others to do good, resulting in an energized, motivated workforce that is committed to building the community as well as the business.

Developing a sense of community through philanthropic efforts is a key component of the Dixon Schwabl culture. Providing opportunities to help others gives employees a sense that they are an integral part of the community, applying their time and energy to worthy causes. The energy and excitement involved in philanthropy makes giving back a win-win exchange for Dixon Schwabl and the community.

Dixon Schwabl provides additional information about the firm on its Web site at www.dixonschwabl.com.

Dixon Schwabl currently works with dozens of not-for-profit organizations in the area:

Al Sigl Center • American Diabetes Association • American Heart Association • The Arc of Monroe County • Bishop Sheen Ecumenical Housing Foundation • Camp DayDreams • Camp Good Days & Special Times • Catholic Family Center • Catholic Schools of the Finger Lakes • Cloverwood Senior Living • Constellation Brands Marvin Sands Performing Arts Center • Daystar • EnCompass Resources for Learning • EquiCenter • ESL Charitable Foundation • Finger Lakes Thoroughbred Adoption Program • Finger Lakes Visitors Connection • Garth Fagan Dance • George Eastman Circle • Gilda's Club Rochester New York • Golisano Children's Hospital at Strong • Greater Canandaigua Family YMCA • Happiness House • Hillside Family of Agencies • Hillside Work-Scholarship Connection • Juvenile Diabetes Research Foundation • Kinship Care Resource • Leukemia & Lymphoma Society Rochester New York Chapter • Lifespan • Mercier Literacy Program • Mercy Flight • Monroe Community College Foundation • National Center for Missing & Exploited Children/New York Branch • New York Wine & Culinary Center • 1941 Historical Aircraft Group Museum • Ontario ARC • Ontario Children's Foundation • Pluta Cancer Center • Polisseni Foundation • Rochester Auto Dealers' Charitable Foundation • Rochester City Ballet • Rochester High Falls International Film Festival • Rochester Museum & Science Center • Rochester Philharmonic Orchestra • St. Bernard's Seminary • St. Mary's School • The Friendly Home • The Sands Academy • F. F. Thompson Foundation • Unity Health System • University of Rochester • Visiting Nurse Service Meals on Wheels • YMCA of Greater Rochester

Above left: The New York Wine & Culinary Center is located in Canandaigua, a richly historical and scenic region of New York state. Dixon Schwabl worked with a team of government, academic, cultural, and travel and tourism leaders to launch the facility, which welcomes thousands of visitors annually to the area. Above right: Rochester is home to a number of world-renowned cultural organizations, including Garth Fagan Dance. Dixon Schwabl works with many arts and cultural not-for-profit organizations, assisting them with strategic marketing and development activities.

PROFILES OF COMPANIES AND ORGANIZATIONS

Professional and Business Services

Dixon Schwabl, Inc.

Founded in 1987, this full-service agency has grown to become one of Rochester's top marketing communications firms, earning national recognition for outstanding communications programs, for its creative work environment, and for making Rochester a great place to work.

Above: Dixon Schwabl, Inc.'s talented team gathers in the building's soaring lobby.

When it comes to turning a good company into a great company, Dixon Schwabl, Inc. can make it happen. In addition to changing the way companies think about internal and external communications, the close-knit, creative team at Dixon Schwabl, headquartered in Rochester, New York, has earned the number one spot among small companies on the 2008 list of the Best Small and Medium Companies to Work for in America compiled by the Great Place to Work Institute in San Francisco, California. The agency's ability to combine the roles of excellent employer, conscientious corporation, and outstanding full-service agency has earned praise from clients and business organizations alike. Among these accolades are the Rochester Business Ethics Award and the Ernst & Young Entrepreneur of the Year Award, Communications Division. With 2007 annual revenues of $126 million, Dixon Schwabl is known for launching powerful campaigns for local and national clients.

Advertising, Marketing, and Public Relations

A one-stop creative shop, Dixon Schwabl has the talent and ideas to produce each with maximum impact. The advertising process begins with a team of imaginative art directors, designers, and copywriters who envision concepts and translate them into highly visible print, outdoor, and transit advertisements, direct mail pieces, television commercials, Web site content, package design, and collateral. Additional communications professionals round out the team: print-production supervisors implement advanced technology; broadcast editors use the company's state-of-the-art audio-video facilities to produce radio and television spots, promotional and training videos, documentaries, and video news releases; and experienced media planners combine research, analysis, negotiation, and buying power to place advertisements.

A smart marketing plan is also key to any new venture or for reviving an established brand or company, and Dixon Schwabl knows how to unlock the possibilities for great success. The firm's knowledgeable account services specialists work with clients to identify strategies—from business-to-business and direct marketing to brand management and special promotions—that are based on thorough market research. Clients trust these Dixon Schwabl specialists to oversee the planning, budgeting, and tactical implementation of a comprehensive marketing plan.

Effective media campaigns are conducted by Dixon Schwabl's public relations specialists. These energetic, persistent, and well-connected experts—with a global reach—ensure that clients are able to communicate their story, products, or important message through media relations, publicity, special events planning and coordination, fund-raisers, public affairs organizations, community relations, crisis communications, employee relations, and the release of public relations research and writings.

Great Leadership Brings Success

At the helm of one of Rochester's great places to work is founder and CEO Lauren Dixon, who has been responsible for the growth and development of the agency from the beginning. By her side is the agency's president and owner Mike Schwabl, who oversees strategic planning, concept and brand development, and creative execution for all accounts and manages in-house broadcast production and engineering.

Named Small-Business Person of the Year by the Greater Rochester Metro Chamber of Commerce, Dixon describes the source of her motivation: "Our goal is to one day have Rochester be known as America's greatest place to work. Helping other companies achieve this will make our city a healthier place and will bring pride to the community," she says. "We are proud to be part of the many companies who have already achieved the 'Great Place to Work' distinction, such as Wegmans, Paychex, Nixon Peabody, Genencor, and others."

Dixon Schwabl's management style serves as a model for a healthy corporate culture. "The more employees feel valued, the more productive and profitable the company will be as a whole," says Dixon. "We encourage our vice presidents, supervisors, and managers to really listen to what our employees need and want and to make decisions accordingly. This may not be easy since these people are usually the ones who are giving the answers."

Listening to employees, however, is just one element in achieving success and maintaining a satisfied workforce, according to Dixon Schwabl, which describes several of the fundamental precepts it adheres to:

- Follow the leaders: Join industry trendsetters who creatively lead the way with cutting-edge technology. Dixon Schwabl's Emerging Technologies and Economic Development Group helps the agency's clients plan for success.
- Become more interactive: Interactive methods expand a company's audience reach and enable greater brand exposure. Dixon Schwabl's team advises clients on dynamic presentations, Web site makeovers, electronic marketing, and online advertising.
- Discover the company's "wow" factor: Know exactly who and what the company stands for. Dixon Schwabl offers a program designed to help clients identify their strengths and weaknesses, areas of opportunity for growth, and potential threats to their brand.
- Cause a sensation: "Cause marketing"—the cooperative efforts of a company and a charitable cause—benefits all parties. Dixon Schwabl assists clients in determining which forms of cause marketing will best serve their needs and create a win-win relationship.
- "Go green": Help save the environment and reduce expenses at the same time through efficient office practices. For Dixon Schwabl, going green includes working with like-minded vendors and saving paper by using more interactive methods.
- Make it work: Establish a healthy corporate culture that attracts top talent and maintains low employee turnover. The agency considers that being a great place to work means establishing effective leadership, listening to employees, and creating a work environment that is fun.
- Impact the community: The agency reminds clients that local involvement draws attention to important issues and can empower the entire region.

For more than 20 years, Dixon Schwabl has helped discover and market the "wow" factor for businesses in Rochester and across the country. Additional information can be found on Dixon Schwabl, Inc.'s Web site at www.dixonschwabl.com.

Both photos: With the slide that connects floors (above left) and the Primal Scream Room (above), Dixon Schwabl creates a work environment that is fun and, therefore, more productive.

Boylan, Brown, Code, Vigdor & Wilson, LLP

For more than 30 years, this Rochester, New York–based law firm has focused on providing efficient, first-rate service to its clients. It has the knowledge, experience, resources, and expertise in business and corporate legal services to help its clients meet challenges and achieve their goals and objectives.

Above: Since its founding in 1974, the firm of Boylan, Brown, Code, Vigdor & Wilson, LLP has grown dramatically in response to the ever more complex needs of its clients, yet its commitment to providing outstanding client service remains unchanged.

Since the firm's founding in 1974, Boylan, Brown, Code, Vigdor & Wilson, LLP has continued to grow and expand to meet the ever-increasing needs of its clients, becoming one of the largest law firms in Rochester. The entrepreneurial spirit that led five young attorneys to leave the security of a well-established firm and start their own practice remains with Boylan Brown today. As the practice of law and the global economic landscape have evolved, so too has Boylan Brown. The firm maintains a dynamic legal practice that evolves in response to its clients' political, social, domestic, and global realities. Boylan Brown remains firmly committed to the Rochester community, while at the same time ensuring that clients receive exceptional advice and service with an international scope.

Client-Centered Practice

Boylan Brown's core value is the ability to help its clients achieve their most important objectives—to create and sustain growth, to protect their assets and interests, and to support the progression of a logical, planned process to achieve key business and personal objectives.

Boylan Brown attorneys provide consultative services to start-up and emerging technology companies that add value to each enterprise and promote growth. The firm has guided many companies through initial structuring, private and public financing rounds, establishment of intellectual property rights, and employment issues. As those companies seek to expand, the firm routinely assists them with mergers and acquisitions, executive compensation, real estate acquisition and development, and corporate governance.

As Boylan Brown's clients expand their businesses, the firm recognizes the need to protect their key assets to ensure both the uninterrupted continuation of business and the future security of those assets for key stakeholders. First and foremost, Boylan Brown attorneys use their experience and foresight to structure contracts and agreements that will withstand any challenges and protect their clients from harm. Should a dispute arise, the firm employs case-by-case analysis and management practices in order to balance their clients' need for vigorous representation and resolution with their need for efficiency and accountability. Whether through litigation, arbitration, mediation, or negotiation, Boylan Brown has the ability and experience to lead to successful conclusion nearly any type of dispute in any industry.

The ultimate goal of any business venture is the creation of wealth for its key stakeholders. Boylan Brown attorneys specialize in wealth succession planning for business owners and provide consultative services to ensure the transition of assets from one phase of ownership to the next and, ultimately, to successive generations. Whether through the sale of a company, a merger, an acquisition, or

the use of other business succession tools such as employee stock ownership plans (ESOPs), Boylan Brown attorneys maximize the value of assets in a company and structure deals that provide the greatest benefit to their clients. They provide personally tailored services to business owners and key stakeholders to preserve and transfer wealth to their family members, including wills, estate and tax planning, family organizations, and a specialized Family Compass program for high-net-worth individuals.

Unique Value Delivery

Boylan Brown has distinguished itself from its competitors through unique perspectives on the way a law firm delivers value to its clients and by redefining the traditional law firm business model to focus on efficiency, innovative practices, and the creation of a deeper value model. That business model is designed around the ever-changing needs of the firm's clients and the increasingly challenging environment in which they live and work.

A crucial component of Boylan Brown's value to its clients is access to the firm's ever-expanding network of trusted professional resources and partner firms who match the firm's standard of excellence in their respective fields. When clients need professional advice in other jurisdictions or in nonlegal areas of expertise, Boylan Brown confidently engages trusted professionals in a variety of organizations of which the firm is a member, including the International Society of Primerus Law Firms, the Alliance of Merger & Acquisition Advisors, the Transatlantic Business Council, and many others. No matter the jurisdiction, industry, or challenge, Boylan Brown provides clients with top-notch advice on their business transactions, both domestic and international.

People Driving Success

The attorneys and staff at Boylan Brown are exceptional in their talent, experience, skill, and diversity. Those qualities are brought together in a team-based approach in order to provide top-notch legal solutions with efficiency, flexibility, professionalism, and incomparable client service. Everyone at Boylan Brown shares a commonality of purpose, a way of conducting themselves individually and as an entire company that defines the firm and supports the growth, protection, and succession of their clients' business and personal assets.

Boylan, Brown, Code, Vigdor & Wilson, LLP provides additional information on its Web site at www.boylanbrown.com.

b BoylanBrown
Growth.Protection.Succession.
BUSINESS AND CORPORATE LAW

Above left: The offices of Boylan Brown are based in Rochester, New York. Above center: The firm is small enough to ensure close attention from partners who are involved in all issues, and yet large enough to ensure that expertise is available in many areas of legal specialization. Above right: With a staff of 37 attorneys, Boylan Brown specializes in such fields as business, corporate and intellectual property law, creditors' rights, real estate, environmental and public law, litigation, tax law, and more.

Harris Interactive

This internationally recognized and highly respected market research company—a full-service research partner with global capabilities—provides surveys, statistics, and opinion polls, among other data, to policy makers, business leaders, and media corporations, helping them to achieve measurable performance improvements.

Above: Harris Interactive became a public company on December 6, 1999 and trades under the symbol HPOL on the Nasdaq stock market.

Harris Interactive®, headquartered in Rochester, New York, is a global leader in custom-tailored market research with offices in North America, Europe, and Asia. With 320 Rochester-based employees and over 1,100 staff members worldwide, including experts in advertising, branding, loyalty, health care, financial services, and technology, Harris Interactive provides innovative research, insights, and strategic advice to assist clients in improving good business results.

The company's rich history in multimodal research began in 1975 with the founding of the Gordon S. Black Corporation by former University of Rochester professor Gordon S. Black, Ph.D. In 1996 the corporation acquired Louis Harris and Associates, the organization established by Lou Harris, pollster for President John F. Kennedy. Subsequent acquisitions have included WirthlinWorldwide, an organization founded by Richard Wirthlin, Ph.D., pollster for President Ronald Reagan; MediaTransfer AG Netresearch and Consulting in Germany; and MarketShare in Asia; among others.

Harris Interactive is widely known for The Harris Poll®, one of the longest-running, independent opinion polls, and as a global leader in online research. The company has one of the world's largest panel of survey respondents—the Harris Poll Online, which is continually enhanced to meet changing client demands. Harris Interactive has now conducted more than 85 million online surveys in 39 languages and in 125 countries around the world.

Harris Interactive's strong science and methodology form the core of its business and separate it from the competition. As an industry leader, Harris Interactive continuously raises the bar by developing innovative research methods to deliver accurate, reliable, and representative data to its clients. The company provides additional information on its Web site at www.harrisinteractive.com.

The demand for trustworthy customized market research continues to grow worldwide, and as a full-service research partner that offers qualitative and quantitative methods as well as traditional and online data collection modes, Harris Interactive prides itself on the ability to recommend and deliver sound research approaches regardless of location. Whether the research opportunity involves a single product, a whole division, or an entire enterprise, Harris Interactive delivers the knowledge that brings power and success.

Harter Secrest & Emery LLP

This longtime law practice has an excellent record of success in providing value and results for its clients—from large multinational corporations to start-up businesses to individuals. The firm's attorneys and counselors offer proactive legal services, with locations now in Rochester, Buffalo, and Albany, New York, and in Naples, Florida.

Harter Secrest & Emery LLP Services

As a full-service law firm, HSE provides a broad range of legal services through collaboration between specialty practice groups, including but not limited to the following:

- Banking and Finance
- Bankruptcy
- Business and Corporate
- Employee Benefits
- Environmental
- Governmental Affairs
- Health Care
- Immigration
- Intellectual Property
- Labor and Employment
- Land Use and Zoning
- Litigation
- Municipal
- Real Estate
- Securities
- Tax
- Telecommunications and Energy
- Trusts and Estates

Harter Secrest & Emery LLP (HSE) is a diverse and dynamic law practice dedicated to providing cost-effective, real-world solutions that achieve its clients' goals. Established in 1893 by James Havens and Nathaniel Foote, HSE continues to practice law in the same manner as its founders—with skill, creativity, and attentiveness.

With offices in Rochester, Buffalo, and Albany, New York, and in Naples, Florida, this full-service firm is composed of more than 130 attorneys and 30 paralegals serving clients in the region and nationally. HSE serves emerging business clients as well as such well-known corporations as American Express, Bausch & Lomb, Paychex, Ultralife, and Eastman Kodak, a client from the firm's earliest days. HSE also has longstanding relationships with valued not-for-profit and educational clients and individuals.

HSE attorneys contribute to the communities they serve. The firm is known for providing pro bono legal services through the Volunteer Legal Services Project in Monroe County and the Volunteer Lawyers Project in Erie County, and for doing community service work through organizations such as Habitat for Humanity, Volunteers of America, and Lawyers for Learning.

HSE attorneys have won many notable cases, including the successful resolution of the first case in the U.S. Western District of New York under the Americans with Disabilities Act; the recovery of more than $250 million in Medicaid reimbursement funding for more than 300 nursing home clients across New York state; and the successful challenge before the U.S. Supreme Court to a federal law regulating radioactive waste. The firm represents a variety of public and private sector clients in State Environmental Quality Review Act proceedings, and is the upstate New York land use and zoning counsel for one of the nation's largest developer/retailers.

Other notable distinctions for HSE include its ranking as the number one law firm to work for in the entire nation in *The American Lawyer* magazine's survey of midlevel associates for three years in a row, from 2004 to 2006, with a continued place in the nation's top 20 in 2007. The firm was also recognized for three years running by the prestigious *Corporate Board Member* magazine, which ranked HSE the number one business law firm in Rochester following its most recent annual surveys of more than 67,000 public company board members and their in-house counsel.

As it has for more than a century, Harter Secrest & Emery LLP continues to provide its clients expert legal counsel, actively partnering with business leaders and entrepreneurs to successfully resolve their varied legal and business challenges.

Above: Harter Secrest & Emery LLP has more than 130 attorneys and 30 paralegals offering services in a wide range of specialties.

Paychex, Inc.

This company is a recognized leader in the payroll, human resource, and benefits outsourcing industry with a steadfast commitment to success and a record of achievement that continues a tradition of delivering excellence. In its more than 35 years of service, the company has expanded from 40 clients to more than 572,000 businesses across the country—and continues to grow.

Above left: Paychex, Inc. headquarters is located in Rochester, New York. Above right: Paychex has eight offices throughout Monroe County, New York, and more than 100 locations across the United States.

Paychex, Inc. was founded in 1971 by B. Thomas Golisano with just $3,000 and a great idea—to make payroll outsourcing easy and affordable for small businesses. Started with just one employee, Paychex now has more than 12,000 employees across the United States, with over 3,000 of those employees located in Rochester, New York—home to the company's headquarters.

Today, Paychex serves more than 572,000 businesses nationwide and in Germany, and offers an ever-growing variety of payroll and human resource products and services that help clients do what they do best—run their business. In 2008, total revenues surpassed $2 billion for the first time in company history. The first billion took more than 30 years to produce, and the second, just five.

With a wide range of services—including payroll processing, retirement services, health insurance, and a fully outsourced human resource solution—Paychex is able to customize its offering to the client's business, whether it is small or large, simple or complicated.

Paychex is continually recognized for its industry-leading products and services. Paychex has consistently been named among the nation's top 401(k) recordkeepers, as ranked by a leading publication dedicated to pension and retirement services. In fact, Paychex administers approximately one in every ten 401(k) plans, according to statistics from the U.S. Department of Labor.

The success of the company goes beyond that of its products and services. The Paychex culture is one focused on its people—the company's biggest asset. Paychex emphasizes the importance of career mobility and training, continued good health for employees and their families, and a healthy work-life balance.

Paychex has earned numerous awards and honors over the years that pay tribute to the company, its people, and its business philosophies. Some of its recognitions being:

- listed among *Fortune*'s "100 Best Companies to Work For";
- included in the Ethisphere Institute's "World's Most Ethical Companies";
- named among "America's Most Admired Companies" by *Fortune*; and
- included among the Top 125 training organizations in the world by *Training* magazine.

Paychex looks to the future with a sense of confidence in its foundation, a commitment to continuing its success through innovative products and services, and staying true to its culture. More information is available at www.paychex.com.

Earnings Statement
354.06
354.06
09/20/2007
09/26/2007

PROFILES OF COMPANIES AND ORGANIZATIONS

Retail and Supermarkets

Wegmans Food Markets, Inc.

Offering high quality goods, a spectacular abundance of choice, restaurant-quality prepared foods, beautiful stores and displays, consistent low prices, and excellent customer service, this supermarket chain is a favorite destination of shoppers in northeastern and mid-Atlantic states.

Above: Wegmans Food Markets, Inc. is a shopper's delight, with beautiful displays of fresh produce, baked goods, seafood, meat, deli products, and international foods, plus everyday groceries and household items.

Wegmans Food Markets, Inc. is a supermarket chain with more than 70 stores in New York, Pennsylvania, New Jersey, Virginia, and Maryland. The family-owned company, founded in 1916, is recognized as an industry leader and innovator. Wegmans has been on *Fortune* magazine's list of the "100 Best Companies to Work For" since 1998, ranking first in 2005. The company has received countless other accolades, including that of "Super Market—the grocery chain that has changed the way we shop" at the 2007 Food Network Awards.

Family Heritage

In the early 1900s, brothers John and Walter Wegman started as pushcart peddlers of fresh produce in their hometown of Rochester, New York. Eventually, the brothers opened shops and Walter's son, Robert B. Wegman, joined the business. In 1930 the Wegmans made national headlines when they opened a 20,000-square-foot store—considerably large by standards of the day—with innovations like vaporized water spray for produce and a 300-seat cafeteria.

Robert became president in 1950, then chairman in 1969, and led the company until his death in April 2006. Today it is headed by CEO Danny Wegman, Robert's son. Colleen Wegman, Danny's daughter, was named president in January 2005. His other daughter, Nicole Wegman, is vice president of wine merchandising.

A History of Innovation

As the company grew, Wegmans introduced many firsts, among the most important being unprecedented levels of care and respect for people—employees, customers, and community members alike. Wegmans was among the first to offer one-stop shopping, a revolutionary concept that created the kind of shopping experience that people now take for granted. Building upon the accomplishments of the first Wegman generation, the next three generations worked to raise the bar, opening bigger and better stores with more products and services, making the company a better place to work, and investing in new technologies that would improve service, save time, or lower costs for customers.

Keeping Pace with the Customers

Wegmans has evolved with its customers. When the demand for organic and natural foods grew in the 1990s, Wegmans created Nature's Marketplace, featuring snacks, entrees, supplements, foods for special dietary needs, and even cosmetics and cleaning products. Organic produce, often from local farms,

shared space with those grown conventionally. Wegmans even pioneered its own organic research farm and introduced a popular line of Wegmans-brand organic products.

When busy families needed help with meals, Wegmans responded with Market Café, a cozy space to enjoy a variety of freshly made foods. More help for busy families includes the Wegmans' Web site (www.wegmans.com), which boasts step-by-step cooking videos, product information, thousands of Wegmans-developed recipes, and an interactive tool that creates grocery lists organized by the aisles of the local Wegmans.

Investing in Employees and the Community

One of Robert's first actions as president was to raise all salaries. Next a broad program of health care benefits was introduced. Later, the company added other benefits, including an employee scholarship program, which has offered more than $60 million in college tuition assistance to more than 20,000 employees since it began in 1984.

In 1987 the company created the Work-Scholarship Connection, a program that successfully reduces the drop-out rate among at-risk students in the Rochester City School District. Now administered by the Hillside Family of Agencies, the program serves nearly 1,500 students. Each student is provided with a youth advocate, a part-time job, and a workplace mentor at Wegmans and other participating companies. This program received the American Business Press Points of Light Award in 1991 from President George Bush.

Wegmans leads the way in community involvement wherever it is. It partners with not-for-profit groups in each market area to address the community's most pressing concerns. Support for United Way is a priority, as is support for programs that reduce hunger, help young people succeed, strengthen neighborhoods, and promote healthy eating. In 1998 the company became the title sponsor of the Wegmans Rochester LPGA tournament.

A Tourist Destination

Grand openings for a new Wegmans means crowds lining up at dawn. People come for the European ambience, the Meal Station coach offering feature recipe samples, and the renowned customer service. Customers are attracted by the freshness of the foods, including artisan breads, cappuccino brewed to order, sushi made within minutes, and hundreds of incredible cheeses. Everything that is needed can be found—even exotic, hard-to-find items. Knowledgeable employees help customers make great meals easy, healthy, and affordable. Wegmans has even become a tourist attraction for many, drawing visitors to experience its wide variety of goods and services.

As Wegmans approaches its 100th anniversary, it can take much of the credit for transforming the grocery shopping experience.

Left: Many Wegmans Food Markets, such as this one in Harrisburg, Pennsylvania, have opened as a response to requests from communities. The company has won dozens of awards and distinctions for making the shopping experience better and for treating customers, employees, and communities in an exemplary manner. Above center: Wegmans offers many customer-convenience services and "stores within a store," such as the chef's case, which features gourmet cold or ready-to-heat entrees, side dishes, and salads. Above right: Wegmans Food Markets is headed by CEO Danny Wegman (center) and his daughters, Nicole Wegman (left), who serves as vice president of wine merchandising, and Colleen Wegman, who serves as president of the company.

PROFILES OF COMPANIES AND ORGANIZATIONS

Technology, Internet, Telecommunications, and Digital Services

Frontier Communications

This company provides advanced telecommunications products and services for businesses and residences in rural and suburban areas in 24 states. It offers local and long-distance telephone services, high-speed Internet access, and satellite television, including digital and wireless options and valuable technical support.

Above: Frontier Communications is one of the nation's largest rural local-exchange carriers, offering local and long-distance telephone service, digital phone service, Dish Network satellite television service, Internet access, and wireless Internet access.

Frontier Communications has deep roots in Rochester, New York. Founded in 1899 as the Home Telephone Co. of Rochester, it was soon renamed the Rochester Telephone Co. In 2008 it became Frontier Communications. Still known as Rochester's telephone company, Frontier is so much more today.

In the telephone sector, Frontier provides local and long-distance services. Many plans and features are offered, including voice mail, caller ID, call waiting, call forwarding, auto call return, and busy signal redial.

For Internet access, Frontier High-Speed Internet Max downloads at speeds up to 10 million bits per second (Mbps). Customers can also choose FrontierNet Dialup. Frontier Internet includes Web-based e-mail with free e-mail addresses along with anti-spam technology and technical support. Antivirus technology is available. Wireless Internet service is offered in a growing number of locations.

For television service, Frontier offers Dish Network satellite TV, with many options for entertainment, sports, and news. Dish Network programming includes dozens of high-definition channels.

For businesses, Frontier can provide high-speed Internet access as well as computer networks, telephone equipment, and data and voice services. Frontier's Peace of Mind plan for residential and business customers supplies automatic hard-drive backup, wireless network setup, technical support, and personal computer security checks and tune-ups.

Frontier's hard-drive backup service preserves data and prevents loss. Before a file leaves the customer's computer, it is encrypted with the kind of secure coding technology used by financial institutions. Data is backed up automatically whenever the customer adds to or modifies files, including text, photos, music, and video files. The files are stored at a secure remote location, and the customer can access them anytime from nearly any computer.

Frontier serves three million access lines and high-speed Internet subscribers in rural and suburban areas in 24 states. Frontier Communications Corporation (NYSE: FTR) is included in the Standard & Poor's 500 Index.

For telephone, television, and Internet services, Frontier offers the features and equipment that customers want and the packages that provide the best buys. As it has from the beginning, Frontier will continue to provide reliable customer service and advanced technologies well into the future.

Additional information about Frontier Communications is available on the company's Web site at www.frontieronline.com.

One Communications

With a wide, dense network footprint throughout the Northeast, mid-Atlantic, and upper Midwest regions of the United States, this company is the largest privately held competitive local exchange carrier (CLEC) in the nation, offering a full complement of advanced telecommunications services.

Above left: The Galileo Room is an award-winning conference space at One Communications headquarters in downtown Rochester, New York. Above right: Engineers closely monitor the company's advanced telecommunications network from its Network Surveillance Center.

Headquartered in Rochester, New York, One Communications provides telecommunications services to more than 160,000 businesses. With annual revenues of over $800 million and more than 2,000 employees, the company provides small-to-midsize companies with voice, data, Internet, and mobility services over an advanced telecommunications network.

In 2006, One Communications was formed through the merging of three successful companies, including Choice One Communications, based in Rochester. Four local entrepreneurs established Choice One in 1998 as an alternative to the larger, incumbent telephone companies. One of the first independent competitive local exchange carriers (CLEC) in the nation, Choice One sprang from the Telecommunications Act of 1996, which was enacted to encourage industry competition. Today, One Communications is the largest privately held CLEC in the United States and has the financial strength to invest in technology while still delivering exceptional value and service.

The dedicated professionals at One Communications work to provide personal attention and custom-tailored solutions to fit the unique requirements of each customer. Its robust product portfolio includes local and long-distance telephone services; high-speed Internet and T1 services; private networking and data services; managed services; Web hosting; and wireless options, making One Communications a single-source provider of both stand-alone and integrated telecommunications services.

One Communications invests in industry-leading technologies throughout its dense, facilities-based network, which consists of an Internet protocol (IP) platform core with 11,000 miles of fiber-optic cable connecting more than 700 unique collocations sites in 16 states and the District of Columbia. The majority of the One Communications network is wholly owned, a distinct competitive advantage in today's telecommunications landscape. The company's Network Surveillance Center monitors its network elements around the clock to ensure outstanding reliability and responsiveness. One Communications provides additional information about its products and services on its Web site (www.onecommunications.com).

The company has several professional sports teams among its client base and maintains corporate partnerships with the Green Bay Packers, Pittsburgh Steelers, Boston Red Sox, Baltimore Orioles, and Philadelphia Soul.

One Communications is dedicated to supporting its communities. Its employees are involved in many charitable organizations throughout its footprint. It has supported such nonprofit organizations as Big Brothers Big Sisters, the Baden Street Settlement, The Community Place of Greater Rochester, Catholic Charities USA, the Center for Youth Services, Northpointe Council, and Fantasy Flight Camps. One Communications is proud to call Rochester home and looks forward to a prosperous future.

PAETEC Holding Corp.

Founded in 1998, this dynamic provider of data, voice, and Internet products and services—with unique value-added offerings—has quickly grown to serve business-class customers in more than 80 percent of the nation's top 100 metropolitan areas. Its tailored solutions and first-rate customer service have helped more than 50,000 businesses nationwide.

Above: A PAETEC technician at the company's Rochester Network Operations Center provides support to a customer.

If PAETEC founder and CEO, Arunas A. Chesonis, were to be asked what the secret is for his company's success, he would probably say it simply comes down to people. For example, hiring and training the most talented employees in the industry. Or driving a near obsession with serving customers. Or observing the principles on treating people in the business book on PAETEC coauthored by Chesonis, *It Isn't Just Business, It's Personal.*

In fact, the unusual moniker PAETEC was coined by two early employees who suggested the acronym for people in Chesonis's family—his wife, Pam, and children, in descending order of age, Adam, Erik, Tessa, and Emma Chesonis.

In just over 10 years, the nationwide telecommunications provider has grown from a small, eight-person company in Fairport to a company with nearly 4,000 employees in 82 of the top 100 metropolitan areas in the United States and more than a billion dollars in annual revenue.

At the essence of the company's identity are four corporate values that are reflected throughout every aspect of the organization: a caring culture, open communication, unmatched service, and personalized solutions. These values have not gone unnoticed. In 2005 PAETEC received the American Business Ethics Award for a midsize business by the Association of Financial Service Professionals. And in 2006, the Genesee Valley Chapter of the Association of Fundraising Professionals honored PAETEC with the Outstanding Corporation award.

PAETEC's values also are manifested in the company's innovative, custom-designed communication solutions for businesses. PAETEC offers a comprehensive suite of data, voice, and Internet protocol (IP) services, as well as enterprise communications management software and telecommunications equipment. Indeed, if a telecommunications solution is helping a business to communicate more efficiently, PAETEC is likely to be involved.

Even with its more than 50,000 business customers, PAETEC continues to demonstrate outstanding service. It strives to ensure that every customer who calls customer care is able to speak with a representative in 20 seconds or less. PAETEC prides itself on merging old-fashioned business values with the newest innovations in technology.

Most notably for people in Rochester, in late 2007 the community-minded company announced plans to build its new corporate headquarters in downtown Rochester on the Midtown Plaza redevelopment site. The move will not only consolidate four Rochester-area buildings into one location but also will bring more than 1,000 employees into downtown Rochester and will serve as part of the comprehensive revitalization plan for the area. PAETEC provides additional information about the company on its Web site at www.paetec.com.

Left: PAETEC strives to answer every call to customer care in 20 seconds or less.

PROFILES OF COMPANIES AND ORGANIZATIONS

Tourism, Entertainment, and Hospitality

Rochester Riverside Convention Center

This state-of-the-art convention center is one of only a few convention centers in the world honored by the Confrérie de la Chaîne des Rôtisseurs, an international society of gastronomes created by King Louis IX in 1248. In addition to its world-class menus and catering, the Rochester Riverside Convention Center features 100,000 square feet of flexible meeting space, outstanding floral and decor services, and excellent customer service.

Above and right: Conveniently located in the heart of Rochester, New York, the Rochester Riverside Convention Center (RRCC) borders the scenic Genesee River. The architecturally stunning facility—offering ample flexible meeting or event space—also features enclosed walkway connections to major hotels and parking garages to shelter guests from the elements.

Rochester Riverside Convention Center (RRCC) has the talent, facilities, and can-do attitude that is necessary to successfully meet the needs of any event—from trade shows, conferences, and corporate meetings to banquets, weddings, and public exhibits. Regardless of the event size, the RRCC's competent staff members are always available to address questions and concerns, handle every detail that requires follow-up, and skillfully orchestrate last-minute changes, thereby giving clients more time to conduct business and focus on the event.

Located on the scenic Genesee River, the RRCC is at the hub of a bustling convention district in the heart of Rochester and is connected to several major hotels by an enclosed skywalk system and riverside walkway. Rochester's high concentration of educational, research, and business organizations can also serve as a valuable resource during corporate meetings and conventions.

Creative Professionals and Excellent Service

When it is not staging high-attendance conventions, the RRCC hosts fundraisers and galas, corporate launches, community events, awards functions, banquets, sales events, annual meetings, employee recognition parties, themed events, rehearsal dinners, bridal showers, wedding ceremonies, and receptions for all faiths.

The built-in flexibility of the RRCC's meeting space also enables the staff to move partitions and staging quickly and easily, providing the most efficient and effective configuration for a specific function. The RRCC excels in handling a variety of technology needs, is extensively wired for easy Internet access, and features state-of-the-art lighting and sound systems.

High Quality Catering

Delicious meals and high quality food service complement the RRCC's attentive professional staff and superior facilities. RRCC catering services are available on-site and off-site from a department that is prepared to make every event a special occasion: cocktail parties, white-glove dinners, old-fashioned picnics, wine-tasting receptions, and casual or formal affairs. Popular venues for off-site catering include the George Eastman House International Museum of Photography & Film, the historic building at the American Association of University Women, the central branch of the Rochester Public Library System, and other unique locations.

Catering equipment is also available, including a wide selection of tables and chairs, beautiful beverage glassware, silverware for formal and informal dining, specialty linens and table skirting, chair covers, and a dance floor. From small intimate gatherings to dinners for 3,500, dining and catering with RRCC is second to none, with all foods freshly prepared.

Hospitality at Its Best

Since RRCC opened in 1985 it has been guided in its success by the business acumen and personable warmth of Executive Director Joe Floreano, CFE, who is also a contributing and admired community member. Floreano's vision and work keep the RRCC busy throughout the year, attracting convention groups that are considering staging their events in larger cities.

Many of these groups have become repeat customers. For example, the New York State Association of Computers and Technology in Education has scheduled its annual event in Rochester since its initial gathering in 2002. Floreano's success in attracting and welcoming far-away clients brings thousands of visitors to the city, with the added benefits of increasing business for nearby vendors, hotels, and related companies.

With a lifetime career in the convention center and hospitality business, Floreano is a 32-year member of the International Association of Assembly Managers and a member of the distinguished Confrérie de la Chaîne des Rôtisseurs. He also holds an Honorary Lifetime membership to the American Culinary Federation Professional Cooks/Chefs Association of Rochester Inc. for his contributions to the hospitality industry. In 2008 Floreano was honored with the Charles A. McElravy Award, the highest honor from the International Association of Assembly Managers. And in 2006 he was presented with the Civic Tourism Award at the 85th meeting of the Greater Rochester Visitors Association.

For additional information, visit the Rochester Riverside Convention Center's Web site at www.rrcc.com.

Rochester Riverside Convention Center's Facilities

- Exhibit space for up to 233 10-foot-by-10-foot booths
- 25 meeting rooms
- Seating for 5,000
- Banquet facilities for up to 3,500
- Modern presentation, entertainment, and multimedia capabilities
- State-of-the-art wiring and communications systems
- Two drive-on truck docks measuring 15,000 square feet
- Drive-on access to Empire Hall
- Convenient floor box locations, 30-foot-by-30-foot grid

Rochester Riverside Convention Center's Services

- Personal floral creations
- Floral centerpieces
- Ice carvings
- Balloon art
- Elegant decor for wedding ceremonies and receptions
- Customized menus
- Indoor and outdoor fireworks
- Confetti explosions
- Laser lighting with sound effects
- Specialty lighting and sound systems

Top: The versatile RRCC offers 100,000 square feet of adaptable meeting and exhibit space to meet the needs of any event. Above: The center's world-class catering department can create the perfect menu for a formal or informal event.

Woodcliff Hotel & Spa

Perched on the highest point in Monroe County near New York's scenic Finger Lakes region, this hotel and spa is a tranquil oasis just minutes from the heart of Rochester. The hotel's hilltop location affords guests peaceful solitude and views of the dynamic Rochester skyline and the verdant Bristol Hills.

Above: The Woodcliff Hotel & Spa is located near Rochester in Fairport, New York.

Opened in 1987 as The Lodge at Woodcliff, in 2007 the 234-room hotel changed its name to Woodcliff Hotel & Spa to better represent the property's role as a home away from home for its diverse clientele of business travelers and upscale leisure guests. Each year the hotel hosts thousands of guests visiting the Rochester area for business or pleasure and stages hundreds of corporate and social events.

Woodcliff Hotel & Spa offers exceptional features and recreational activities, from decadent dining in the acclaimed Horizons Restaurant, to luxurious services in Spa Elan, and golfing at the Woodcliff Golf Course. The hotel's venues attract both hotel guests and members of the community.

Horizons Restaurant serves imaginative cuisine with an emphasis on fresh, regional ingredients. Patrons enjoy expansive views while seated in an environment of elegance, with linen-draped tables and comfortable tapestried chairs. The restaurant serves breakfast, lunch, dinner, and on Sunday, an acclaimed brunch. On weekends, Horizons Lounge provides diners with live performances by local jazz entertainers.

Opened at the hotel in April 2005, Spa Elan affords an opportunity for relaxation and indulgence, with a full line of spa treatments, salon services, and boutique products. The spa's soft earth tones, white maple accents, and gentle natural lighting prepare each guest for spiritual renewal and physical refreshment from the moment he or she enters the Spa Elan lobby. In addition to a range of signature body treatments and massages, facials, manicures, pedicures, and other salon services, the spa also offers a menu of express treatments designed to fit relaxation into the schedule of any guest.

Guests seeking more active entertainment can play a round or two of golf at the nine-hole regulation course, complete with golf carts. Spacious indoor heated and seasonal outdoor swimming pools as well as a heated whirlpool spa ensure that guests can enjoy water activities year-round. In summer, a poolside patio becomes a haven for sunbathers and a site for social gatherings.

The hotel's health and fitness center features a variety of cardiovascular and strength training circuit equipment, as well as free weights, a sauna, lockers, and showers. Professional instructors are available for consultation and fee-based, one-on-one training. Outdoor enthusiasts have direct access to the scenic Crescent Trail, which winds for nine miles through gentle hills.

More than 6,000 square feet of meeting space for functions has made Woodcliff Hotel & Spa a premier Rochester-area destination for conferences, business meetings, and social events. At 3,060 square feet, the Conference Center accommodates up to 200 people. Each of four Finger Lakes meeting rooms, at 525 square feet per room, can accommodate gatherings of 40 people. Floor-to-ceiling windows provide energizing natural light in the hotel's event space. Smaller

events and business meetings take place in the Seneca executive boardroom, which hosts up to 12 people, and the Pittsford meeting room, which accommodates up to 18 people. State-of-the-art audiovisual equipment is available, utilizing ceiling-mounted, retractable projection screens, camera, and "smart" lecturn.

A dedicated team of professional conference and event planners works closely with each event's organizers. Full banquet and catering services are available, with extensive menus that cater to the guest's or client's needs, along with a meticulously selected award-winning wine list.

At Woodcliff Hotel & Spa, 234 deluxe guest rooms, including 12 suites with whirlpool spas, offer distinctive style and full modern amenities. Business travelers find an ideal combination of leading-edge technical services, focus-enhancing privacy, and proximity to Rochester's centers of commerce. The hotel's 24-hour business center provides a color copier, fax machine, and personal computer (PC) and printer, and wireless Internet access is available throughout the hotel.

Woodcliff Hotel & Spa is a vital part of the community, employing more than 230 people and taking an active role in local charitable efforts. A longtime supporter of United Way of Greater Rochester, the hotel's annual employee donation campaign has repeatedly been recognized as outstanding for its generosity. Each holiday season, Woodcliff staff members donate toys and other gifts to the Society for the Protection and Care of Children. The hotel's human resources director is committed to creating an environment of care and compassion among the staff. The Woodcliff staff members are highly charitable and donate or lend a helping hand when needed. Some of the beneficiaries of the hotel's community involvement include Special Olympics New York–Genesee Region; Dimitri House, which helps the homeless with emergency food and shelter; and the Epilepsy Foundation of Rochester-Syracuse-Binghamton's annual Chocolate Ball. More information about the hotel is available at www.woodcliffhotelspa.com.

Left: Guests of the Woodcliff Hotel & Spa are welcomed into an atmosphere of comfort, amenities, and warm, personal service expected of a first-class hotel and spa. Above: Affording expansive views, Horizons Restaurant serves breakfast, lunch, dinner, and a Sunday brunch. The adjoining Horizons Lounge serves beverages, meals, and snacks and features live entertainment on weekends.

VisitRochester

This organization helps heighten visitor awareness of the greater Rochester region, an area that offers cosmopolitan urban excitement amidst charming neighborhoods and historic canal towns. Accented by exquisite parks and gardens, Rochester has a rich history reflected in striking architecture, a world-class arts and culture scene, exciting international festivals, and abundant recreational activities.

Above and opposite page: VisitRochester highlights greater Rochester's wonderful attractions.

A Long History

Since 1932 Rochester visitors and convention delegates have been welcomed and assisted by a professional visitors' organization. The Rochester Convention and Publicity Bureau was created by a group of civic-minded individuals who saw the value of convention and visitor business. Now recognized as VisitRochester, the organization continues the founders' vision—beyond all expectations. VisitRochester is Monroe County's official tourism promotion agency. Its mission is to promote Rochester as a preferred destination for meetings, conventions, and leisure travel. The organization promotes Rochester and Monroe County's mix of world-class arts and culture, recreation, sports, entertainment, and first-class visitor amenities.

An Economic Driver

According to a report commissioned by the New York State Department of Economic Development's Division of Tourism, the research firm Tourism Economics indicated that the economic impact of nearly 2 million visitors in Monroe County and Greater Rochester in 2007 was $965.255 million. That impact is expected to reach $1 billion by 2009.

Champion of the Tourism and Hospitality Industry

In 2007 VisitRochester became the first destination-marketing organization (DMO) in New York State to receive a certificate of accreditation from Destination Marketing Association International. In earning this accreditation, a DMO communicates to its community, buyers, and potential visitors that the organization has attained a significant measure of excellence. VisitRochester is proud to be a leader in the state's tourism and hospitality industry.

A Place to Meet

VisitRochester actively recruits meeting and convention business by working with local individuals who hold positions with regional, state, national, and international organizations. Its sales department gratefully acknowledges the assistance of these individuals, who help promote the community's exceptional educational presence, as well as leading-edge technology in biomedical, fuel cell, and optics research. The community's rich cultural resources such as photography, music, and history, including women's history and the Underground Railroad, make it an especially attractive destination for these affinity groups.

Additionally, working with the Monroe County Sports Commission, VisitRochester provides services and assistance to the many outstanding amateur championships, sports-related clinics, and sporting events held in the area each year.

Engaging the Community

Rochester
Made for living®

VisitRochester is also the manager of the community's brand, "Rochester. Made for Living™." The brand was developed by a number of community thought leaders to promote the community's high quality of life and to enhance local residents' recognition of its many attributes.

Additional information about VisitRochester and the greater Rochester region is available at www.visitrochester.com.

E. J. Del Monte Corporation

This company is the builder, owner, and operator of Marriott hotels in cities across New York state, including Rochester, Albany, and Binghamton, and is dedicated to providing the highest-quality service to guests at each of its locations. Using its manufacturing expertise, the company pioneered the development of a building system that incorporates precision monolithic concrete-room castings.

Right: The E. J. Del Monte Corporation's Marriott hotels are luxury establishments that provide comfort and full amenities for business and leisure travelers. The Rochester Marriott Airport Hotel features Revive (as shown), the new bed from Marriott.

The E. J. Del Monte Corporation (EJD)—originally a manufacturer of generators—was founded in 1953 in Rochester, New York, by Ernest J. Del Monte, who remains the company's CEO today. Next, the company applied its expertise to manufacturing equipment used in making precast concrete rooms for buildings, and in 1958 it began a construction and real estate development division.

During the 1970s, EJD patented a precast concrete modular system known as the Delcrete Building Systems. Today the company's building systems are used in a variety of structures, including hotels, apartment buildings, hospitals, and extended-care and correctional facilities throughout the United States, the Middle East, and the Pacific Rim.

EJD constructed a hotel of its own in 1973, the Depot Motor Inn in Pittsford, New York, and in 1974 the company began what has now become a long-standing relationship with hotelier Marriott International. EJD entered the field of hotel management and operation when it opened its first Marriott hotel—the 304-room Rochester Marriott Thruway Hotel, which today is named the RIT Inn and Conference Center.

Over the course of the 1990s, EJD undertook a period of rapid expansion and added 16 more hotels to its portfolio. These included the Renaissance, Courtyard, Residence Inn, and Fairfield Inn brands.

The company's 17 hotels are spread throughout New York state, with nine of its hotels in the Rochester area, and EJD plans to establish hotels at more sites. The corporation provides additional information on its Web site (www.ejdcorp.com).

In both 1998 and 2000, EJD was honored with the Partnership Circle Award from Marriott International as the leading Marriott franchise in the country. The award is based on innovation, outstanding guest satisfaction, consistent performance, and excellent service.

The year 2000 also heralded EJD's first luxury hotel with the opening of The Del Monte Lodge in Pittsford. The following year, Marriott International designated The Del Monte Lodge a Renaissance Hotel. EJD developed and opened its first spa—the Spa at The Del Monte—in 2004.

The E. J. Del Monte Corporation remains dedicated to delivering the highest-quality service to its guests, now and in the future.

Cherbo Publishing Group

Cherbo Publishing Group's business-focused, art book–quality publications, which celebrate the vital spirit of enterprise, are custom books that are used as high-impact economic development tools to enhance reputations, increase profits, and provide global exposure for businesses and organizations.

Both pages, all: Cherbo Publishing Group produces custom books for historical, professional, and government organizations. These fine publications promote the economic development of America's cities, regions, and states by chronicling their history—the people, enterprises, industries, and organizations that have made them great.

Jack Cherbo, Cherbo Publishing Group president and CEO, has been breaking new ground in the sponsored publishing business for more than 40 years.

"Previously, the cost of creating a handsome book for business developments or commemorative occasions fell directly on the sponsoring organization," Cherbo says. "My company pioneered an entirely new concept—funding these books through the sale of corporate profiles."

Cherbo honed his leading edge in Chicago, where he owned a top advertising agency before moving into publishing. Armed with a degree in business administration from Northwestern University, a mind that never stopped, and a keen sense of humor, Cherbo set out to succeed—and continues to do just that.

Cherbo Publishing Group (CPG), formerly a wholly owned subsidiary of Jostens, Inc., a Fortune 500 company, has been a privately held corporation since 1993. CPG is North America's leading publisher of quality custom books for commercial, civic, historical, and trade associations. Publications range from hardcover state, regional, and commemorative books to softcover state and regional business reports. The company is headquartered in Encino, California, and operates regional offices in Philadelphia, Minneapolis, and Houston.

About CPG Publications

CPG has created books for some of America's leading organizations, including the U.S. Chamber of Commerce, Empire State Development, California Sesquicentennial Foundation, Chicago O'Hare International Airport, and the Indiana Manufacturers Association. Participants have included Blue Cross Blue Shield, DuPont, Toyota, Northrop Grumman, and Xerox.

CPG's series range from history books to economic development/relocation books and from business reports to publications of special interest. The economic development series spotlights the outstanding economic and quality-of-life advantages of fast-growing cities, counties, regions, or states. The annual business reports provide an economic snapshot of individual cities, regions, or states. The commemorative series marks milestones for corporations, organizations, and professional and trade associations.

To find out how CPG can help you celebrate a special occasion, or for information on how to showcase your company or organization, contact Jack Cherbo at 818-783-0040, extension 26, or visit www.cherbopub.com.

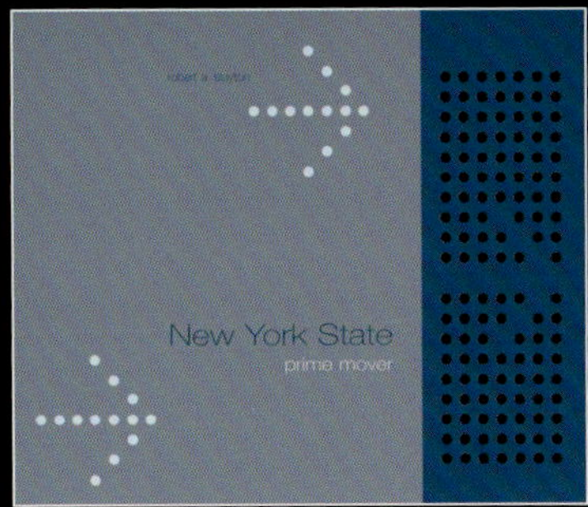

Select CPG Publications

VISIONS OF OPPORTUNITY
City, Regional, and State Series

ALABAMA *The Progress, The Promise*

AMERICA & THE SPIRIT OF ENTERPRISE
Century of Progress, Future of Promise

AURORA, ILLINOIS *A City Second to None*

CALIFORNIA *Golden Past, Shining Future*

CHATTANOOGA *The Renaissance of a City*

CINCINNATI *Bridges to the Future*

CONNECTICUT *Chartered for Progress*

DELAWARE *Incorporating Vision in Industry*

FORT WORTH *Where the Best Begins*

GREATER PHOENIX *Expanding Horizons*

JACKSONVILLE *Where the Future Leads*

LEHIGH VALLEY *Crossroads of Commerce*

MICHIGAN *America's Pacesetter*

MILWAUKEE *Midwestern Metropolis*

MISSOURI *Gateway to Enterprise*

NASHVILLE *Amplified*

NEW YORK STATE *Prime Mover*

NORTH CAROLINA *The State of Minds*

OKLAHOMA *The Center of It All*

PITTSBURGH *Smart City*

SOUTH DAKOTA *Pioneering the Future*

TOLEDO *Access. Opportunity. Edge.*

UTAH *Life Elevated*

WEST VIRGINIA *Reaching New Heights*

WISCONSIN *A Tradition of Innovation*

LEGACY Commemorative Series

ALBERTA AT 100 *Celebrating the Legacy*

BUILD IT & THE CROWDS WILL COME
Seventy-Five Years of Public Assembly

CELEBRATE SAINT PAUL
150 Years of History

DAYTON *On the Wings of Progress*

THE EXHIBITION INDUSTRY
The Power of Commerce

IDAHO *The Heroic Journey*

MINNEAPOLIS *Currents of Change*

NEW JERSEY *Crossroads of Commerce*

NEW YORK STATE ASSOCIATION OF FIRE CHIEFS
Sizing Up a Century of Service

ROCHESTER, MINNESOTA
Transforming the World: Rochester at 150

VIRGINIA
Catalyst of Commerce for Four Centuries

VISIONS TAKING SHAPE
Celebrating 50 Years of the Precast/ Prestressed Concrete Industry

ANNUAL BUSINESS REPORTS

MINNESOTA REPORT *2007*

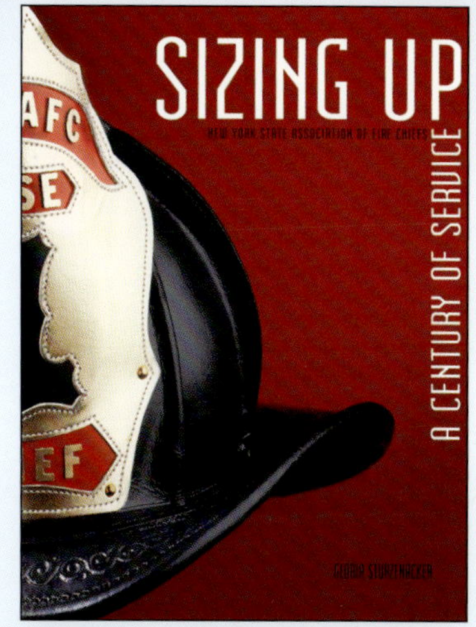

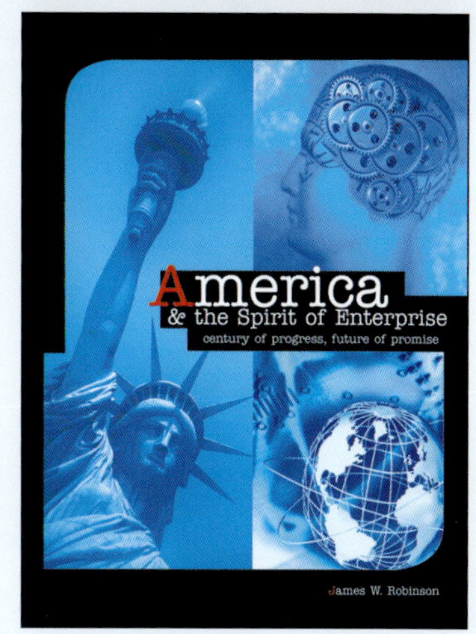

PHOTO CREDITS

Page ii: © Richard Cummins
Page v: © Sheridan Vincent
Page vi: © Sheridan Vincent
Page viii, left: © Paul Van Hoy II/Fotoimpressions
Page ix, left: © Paul Van Hoy II/Fotoimpressions
Page ix, right: © Richard P. Wersinger
Page x: © David Duprey/AP Photo
Page xi, left: © Paul Van Hoy II/Fotoimpressions
Page xi, right: © Doug Wilson/Alamy
Page xii: Courtesy, Rochester Contemporary Art Center
Page xiii: © Andy Olenick
Page xiv: © Lise Gagne
Page xvi: © Arne Thaysen
Page xviii: © A. Sue Weisler/RIT
Page xix: Courtesy, The College at Brockport, State University of New York
Page xx: © 20 Toe Photo
Page xxi, left: © James Lemass
Page xxi, right: © Don Heupel/AP Photo
Page xxii: © Richard Cummins
Page 2, left: From the Collection of the Rochester Public Library Local History Division
Page 2, right: Courtesy, I. N. Phelps Stokes Collection, Miriam and Ira D. Wallach Division of Art, Prints and Photographs, The New York Public Library, Astor, Lenox and Tilden Foundations
Page 3, left: © Underwood & Underwood/Corbis
Page 3, right: © Bettmann/Corbis
Page 4, left: From the Collection of the Rochester City Hall Photo Lab
Page 4, right: © Reuters/Corbis
Page 5, left: From the Collection of the Rochester City Hall Photo Lab
Page 5, right: © Richard Cummins
Page 6: © Sheridan Vincent
Page 8: © Richard Cummins
Page 9: © David Duprey/AP Photo
Page 10, left: © Paul Van Hoy II/Fotoimpressions
Page 10, right: © Paul Van Hoy II/Fotoimpressions
Page 11: © Paul Van Hoy II/Fotoimpressions
Page 12, top: © Gelfand-Piper Photography
Page 12, bottom: © Basil Childers
Page 13: © Paul Van Hoy II/Fotoimpressions
Page 14: © Paul Van Hoy II/Fotoimpressions
Page 15: Courtesy, VisitRochester
Page 16: © Paul Van Hoy II/Fotoimpressions
Page 17, bottom left: © Pete Thompson
Page 17, right: © Doug Wilson/Alamy
Page 18, left: © Tina Manley/North America/Alamy
Page 18, right: Courtesy, Constellation Brands
Page 19, right: © Doerte Mahanay
Page 20, left: Courtesy, Rochester Redwings
Page 21: © 20 Toe Photo
Page 22, top: © Paul Van Hoy II/Fotoimpressions
Page 22, bottom: © Paul Van Hoy II/Fotoimpressions
Page 23: © Paul Van Hoy II/Fotoimpressions
Page 24: © Mike Agiolo/Photo Researchers, Inc.
Page 25: Courtesy, Reflexite Display Optics
Page 26: Courtesy, XLI Corporation
Page 27, left: © Andy Sacks/Getty Images
Page 27, right: © Klaus Lahnstein/Getty Images
Page 28, left: Courtesy, Vaccinex, Inc.
Page 28, right: Courtesy, University of Rochester
Page 29: © A. Sue Weisler/RIT
Page 30: © Paul Van Hoy II/Fotoimpressions
Page 31: © Ian Hooton/Photo Researchers, Inc.
Page 32: Courtesy, Rochester Precision Optics
Page 33: Courtesy, Carestream Health, Inc.
Page 34: © David Duprey/AP Photo
Page 35: © Karen Maze
Page 36, left: © Getty Images
Page 36, right: Courtesy, Bausch & Lomb
Page 37, left: © Karen Maze

Page 37, right: Courtesy, Diamond Packaging
Page 38, left: Courtesy, Animatics Corp.
Page 39, left: Courtesy, Parker Hannifin
Page 39, right: © Getty Images
Page 40, left: Courtesy, Alstom Signaling, Inc.
Page 41, left: Courtesy, Pictometry
Page 41, right: © Kevin Rivoli/AP Photo
Page 42: Courtesy, Wegmans Food Markets
Page 43: © Paul Van Hoy II/Fotoimpressions
Page 44: Courtesy, University of Rochester
Page 45: © Dennis Degnan/Corbis
Page 46, left: Courtesy, University of Rochester
Page 46, right: Courtesy, Rochester Institute of Technology
Page 47: Courtesy, The College at Brockport, State University of New York
Page 48: Courtesy, Monroe Community College
Page 49, left: Courtesy, Roberts Wesleyan College
Page 49, right: Courtesy, Colgate Crozer College
Page 50: Courtesy, University of Rochester Medical Center
Page 51: Courtesy, University of Rochester Medical Center
Page 52, left: © Ben Edwards/Getty Images
Page 53: Courtesy, Unity Health System
Page 54: © Paul Van Hoy II/Fotoimpressions
Page 55: © Stefan Klein
Page 56, left: © Jason Dewey/Getty Images
Page 56, right: © Paul Van Hoy II/Fotoimpressions
Page 57: Courtesy, The Sagamore on East, A Christa Companies Development
Page 58, left: Courtesy, Christenson Corporation
Page 58, right: © Sheridan Vincent
Page 59, right: © Paul Van Hoy II/Fotoimpressions
Page 60, left: © Paul Van Hoy II/Fotoimpressions
Page 61, left: © Paul Van Hoy II/Fotoimpressions
Page 61, right: Courtesy, Clark Patterson Lee
Page 62, left: © Aldo Murillo
Page 62, right: © Getty Images
Page 63: Courtesy, Paychex
Page 64: © Max Schulte
Page 65: © Kevin Law/Jupiter Images
Page 66, left: © A. Sue Weisler/RIT
Page 66, right: Courtesy, Western New York Energy
Page 67, right: Courtesy, Genencor
Page 68, left: Courtesy, Cornell Agriculture & Food Technology Park
Page 68, right: © Mark Evans
Page 69, left: Courtesy, Gleason Corporation
Page 69, right: © Richard Cummins
Page 70: © Paul Van Hoy II/Fotoimpressions
Page 71, left: Courtesy of Genesee & Wyoming Inc.
Page 71, right: © Sheridan Vincent
Page 72: © Lise Gagne
Page 73: © David Nevala/Getty Images
Page 74: Ryan McVay/Photodisc
Page 76: © Penny Clark
Page 80: © Alessandro Terni
Page 85: © Bart Coenders
Page 86: © Tim Pannell/Corbis
Page 92: © Tim Pohl
Page 96: © Christine Balderas
Page 106: © Ingram Publishing/Purestock
Page 110: © Alvaro Heinzen
Page 117: © Clark Todd
Page 121: Courtesy, Eastman Kodak Company
Page 122: © Mike Bentley
Page 126: © Zsolt Nyulaszi
Page 135: © Atanas Bezov
Page 136: © Rob Melnychuk/Digital Vision
Page 140: © Nikolai Okhitin
Page 143: © Edward Rozzo/Corbis
Page 145: © Photodisc
Page 148: © Photodisc
Page 157: © Eric Audras/Photo Alto

cherbo publishing group, inc.

TYPOGRAPHY

Principal faces used: Univers, designed by Adrian Frutiger in 1957;
Helvetica, designed by Matthew Carter, Edouard Hoffmann,
and Max Miedinger in 1959

HARDWARE

Macintosh G5 desktops, digital color laser printing with Xerox Docucolor 250, digital
imaging with Creo EverSmart Supreme

SOFTWARE

QuarkXPress, Adobe Illustrator, Adobe Photoshop, Adobe Acrobat, Microsoft Word,
Eye-One Pro by Gretagmacbeth, Creo Oxygen, FlightCheck

PAPER

Text Paper: #80 Luna Matte

Bound in Rainbow® recycled content papers from
Ecological Fibers, Inc.

Dust Jacket: #100 Sterling-Litho Gloss